Winning Interview Answers for First-time Job Hunters

Denise Taylor

For Simon, provider of love, support and a clean house

For Tom and Nika at the start of their career journey

Winning Interview Answers for First-time Job Hunters

This first edition published 2009
by Trotman Publishing, an imprint of Crimson Publishing,
Westminster House, Kew Road, Richmond, Surrey TW9 2ND

©Trotman Publishing 2009

Author: Denise Taylor

British Library Cataloguing in Publication Data
A catalogue record of this book is available from the British Library.

ISBN: 978-1-84455-206-1

Typeset by RefineCatch Limited, Bungay, Suffolk

Printed and bound in the UK by TJ International Ltd, Padstow,
Cornwall

Contents

Introduction		**5**
1	**I have an interview–what will happen?**	**7**
	Why companies use interviews	7
	How you can prepare	9
	The people you will meet	13
	When you arrive	14
	First impressions	16
2	**What will I be asked?**	**18**
	The order of questions	19
	The different types of questions	19
	The style of questions	22
	Preparing yourself	23
3	**Introductory questions**	**24**
	Opening questions	25
	Who you are	27
4	**Questions about the company and the job**	**33**
	Why this job?	34
	Why us?	36
	What interests you about the products and services?	38
	Why should we offer you this job? Why does this job interest you?	38
	Your ideal job	44
5	**Competency questions (about your experience and skills)**	**45**
	What are competency based questions?	45
	The need for specific rather than general examples	46
	Why you should use the STAR approach	47
	How to prepare for competency based questions	49
	How to answer competency based questions	54

6 Task based questions **64**
Situational questions/hypothetical questions 64
Group interviews 66
Practical exercises 67
Presentations 69
Written exercises 70
Research challenges 70
Group discussion 71

7 Questions about you **73**
Hobbies and interests 73
Working with others 75
Questions about your personal qualities 77
Strengths and weaknesses 78
Questions about your education 85
Flexibility and ability to get to work on time 87
Future plans and goals 88

8 Questions you can ask **90**
Why you need to ask questions 90
What not to ask 91
A plan for how to develop questions 91
How to use questions to emphasise your strengths 93
A great finale to the interview 93

9 Dealing with weak spots in your application **95**
You don't really know what the job involves 95
You lack relevant experience 96
You don't know much about the industry/company 98
When it's a few months since you left school/college
     and you haven't had a job 99

10 After the interview **100**
Post interview review 100
Follow up with thank-you letter 107
Waiting 110
Decision making 110
What to do if you get a regret letter 110
You've got the job 112

One last thing … **114**

Introduction

I want to help you perform well at interview. Too many young people fail to do themselves justice – they don't 'sell' themselves at interview and answer questions in a general, rather than in a specific way. This results in the disappointment of a reject letter as the job they want goes to someone else.

I'm an experienced career coach and I work with a range of clients including younger people, helping them to perform well at interview and get the job they want.

When we first start looking for a job we need to put together a CV or complete an application form, both designed to let a future employer know a bit about us, what we have studied, our hobbies and interests and details on any work experience. We then send it to the company with a letter explaining why we are interested in a particular job. This can seem like a lot of work and we need to take quite a bit of time to make the layout look good and to make sure everything relevant is included.

So it's great news to get a letter or phone call saying that we have reached the interview stage, but it can also be a bit scary, wondering what is going to happen and looking for ways to keep nerves in check.

This book is part of the Winning Series alongside *Winning CVs for First-time Job Hunters*, *Winning Covering Letters for First-time Job Hunters* and *Winning Interviews for First-time Job Hunters*. The first step to getting a job is a great CV sent with a targeted covering letter; once you get short-listed you need to understand the interview process. This book focuses almost exclusively on how to answer questions. You'll get to understand the questions you could be asked and how to respond, with lots of example answers included.

I have written this book to be practical. We'll start with a reminder of the important aspects of interviews and then go into the detail of specific types of interview questions you will be asked, and how to reply, followed by the questions you can ask. Finally you will learn the ways you can enhance your chance of success after the interview via sending a follow up letter, seeking feedback and also how to review your performance so you can learn for next time.

The transition from education to work is one of the biggest life changes you will face. This book will help you to get your first job and start you on your way to a career that is just right for you.

Good luck

Denise Taylor
www.amazingpeople.co.uk

1

I have an interview – what will happen?

Well done! Many people apply for jobs and it is an achievement to be short-listed for interview. You have done well to get this far – you must have submitted a good application and the company are impressed enough to invite you to interview. You may think you are an excellent match for the job, so why would you not get the job offer; but no selection is a formality and no matter what people tell you, you must be well prepared. This is where this book will help.

This chapter will ensure you feel comfortable with the structure of an interview. By the end of it you will be clear on:

- why companies use interviews
- how you can prepare
- the people you will meet
- when you arrive
- first impressions.

Why companies use interviews

Companies use interviews as a means of selecting the best person to do the job. They have details on you from your application form or CV and cover letter, but will you live up to what you have included there? Many people get help with applying for a job so the company want to see how well you can answer questions, and some of these will mean you need to think on your feet; that is why you must do careful preparation.

The recruitment process

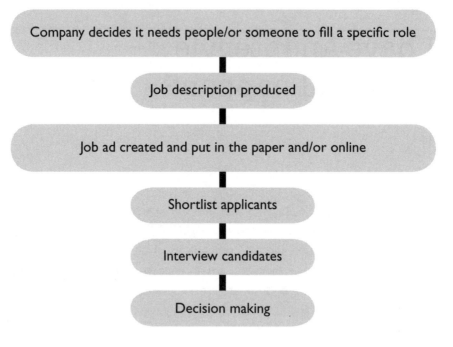

Company decides it needs people/or someone to fill a specific role

Job description produced

Job ad created and put in the paper and/or online

Shortlist applicants

Interview candidates

Decision making

1 The company has **identified the need for a new member of staff** – either because they have a vacancy, somebody has left or got promoted or because there is so much work that they need more staff.

2 The company produces a **job description**, which tells people what they need to do in the job, and also a person specification, which outlines the essential and desirable characteristics of the person. This information is used to **create a job ad** and usually sent out to help people to apply for the job. Please be aware that the bigger the company the more detailed approach is usually taken, often a small independent shop for example will not have much written down.

3 The company will then **short-list** on the basis of people's application. Some companies will decide to interview perhaps four people for one job, other companies may have so many good people apply that it is difficult to make a decision and so may opt for a preliminary stage before the face to face interviews. This could be done by sending you a list of questions to answer by email (Chapter 5 on competency based questions will be very useful preparation for you) or

by conducting phone interviews. All of the information throughout this book will help with the phone interview; but the most important thing to remember is that they can't see you, so you must sound enthusiastic in the replies that you give.

4 Once they have decided who to bring along to the **interview** they will contact candidates by letter, email or even a phone call. Do make sure to get details on where the interview will take place and make sure you know where you are going. It is often worth doing a trial run so you don't get lost and end up late. Make sure you know where to park if you drive and have change available in case you need to pay for car parking.

5 Finally the company decides who gets the **job offer**.

BE WELL PREPARED

Do **read the letter carefully** as there will be plenty of useful information. You may be told the name of the person who will be interviewing you so you can look them up – both on the company web site and also via an Internet search such as Google. You may find out something very useful about them (such as they won employee of the month, or have spoken at a conference) and you can possibly make a reference to this at the interview – perhaps asking them about the conference or praising them on winning their award.

The letter may also tell you more about what will happen. It could be an interview with more than one person – and a panel interview could be with three or more people. Please don't be alarmed by this. The key point to remember is to always look at the person who asks you the question when you reply, and then look around at the other people in the room with a slow sweep.

How you can prepare

Preparation includes mental and physical preparation and also preparing answers to probable questions.

1 Mental preparation

Mental preparation concerns the inner talk we all have – we can say positive and encouraging things that support our belief that we can do well, but what many people do is to have a less than positive self talk, with a conversation running through their head that reminds them of all the reasons why they won't be successful – things like 'why would I get the job', 'I'm really bad at interviews', 'I haven't got any relevant work experience, they must have made a mistake in short-listing me.'

> The company will not have made a mistake! You have been short-listed because they know that you match up on paper with what they are looking for, and now they want to meet with you.

So if you find these negative thoughts going through your head there are ways to deal with them. One way is to visualise a large red stop sign, and when you think of a reason why you won't get the job say **Stop** and change your focus to something else. Another technique is to challenge these thoughts by saying something different. So when the voice in your head says

> 'I haven't got any relevant work experience; they must have made a mistake in short-listing me.'

you can challenge this statement by saying something like:

> 'The company is impressed by my education and my hobbies and interests and I will discuss these with enthusiasm when we meet.'

And if you hear the voice in your head say:

> 'Why would I get the job?'

you can challenge this by saying

> 'Who am I not to get the job?! I've got plenty of interesting things to talk to the interviewer about and I completed a very good application form.'

Believe in yourself – whether you think you can or you can't you are right!

2 Physical preparation

Physical preparation includes things such as:

- how you talk
- voice tone
- your posture and
- remembering to breathe!

How you talk

We all talk but have you ever listened to yourself, or got some accurate feedback from other people? In an interview situation which is seen as quite stressful our voice may often change from what it is usually like, so instead of talking in a normal tone we often find ourselves talking more quietly and sometimes squeaks come out so we sound more like a mouse than a confident young person. This is when practicing answers to questions can help.

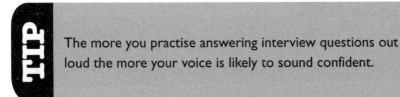

The more you practise answering interview questions out loud the more your voice is likely to sound confident.

There is also a tendency for people to rush though their answer – talking so fast that the interviewer can't grasp what they have to say, so take your time and speak more slowly, putting emphasis on certain words.

We can often have a tendency to say 'umm's', and 'you know's' and other such phrases – we are often not aware of doing these and sometimes when my husband listens to me on the phone he points out that I add 'err's' into my sentences when I'm thinking, so be conscious of it and try to cut out some of these.

Voice tone

It really is important to convey enthusiasm in your voice so don't just say that 'my interests include playing football', but instead say something like 'I *love* playing football' with a more enthusiastic rather than a flat tone.

However well thought through your answers to questions, most interviewers will make a final decision based on your enthusiasm and keenness to do the job. Of course you need to have answered the questions well, but when a decision is between two candidates, it is the one who has demonstrated enthusiasm and keenness that is most likely to get the job. This is not just enthusiasm without any substance, it is enthusiasm based on knowing who you are and why you want the job.

Posture

Posture is about how you stand and sit! You know how your parents have probably moaned at you to stand up straight and not to slouch; well an interviewer expects the same. They expect people to walk confidently into the room – not to walk in with an apologetic air. By the time you have finished working through this book you will be feeling confident and this should show in how you enter a room. Posture is also concerned with how you sit.

ACTION

Sit down on a straight chair as if you are in an interview and get some feedback from others on how you look to them.

It's tempting to slouch, and also to sit with your limbs wide spread. The interview is not the time for you to sit with your legs as far apart as possible; no matter how comfortable this makes you feel. You really need to sit with your legs close together, and your arms neatly near to your body, not floundering around.

Breathing

Finally, breathing; of course we all breathe, but have you ever thought about your breathing? When we are nervous we tend to breathe shallower, so we take in air but all the breathing is done at the top of our chest, not deep in our diaphragm. When we notice this happening we need to breathe slowly and deeply, not only does it get more oxygen through to our brain but it will also mean that we feel less nervous. I always recommend to my clients that they focus on their breathing and consciously count in for 8, hold for 4 and out for 16 as they walk to the interview and at any other time that they feel nervous. Why not try now – slowly breathe in through your nose and out through your mouth. Doing it a few times can really help.

3 Preparing answers to questions

I'm not going to go into a great deal of detail on this here, as this is the focus of the book. What is good to know is that by the time you have carefully read all subsequent chapters, including doing the exercises, you will be feeling confident on answering most of the questions that an interviewer could ask you. So many interview books just touch the surface of how to answer interview questions, but here you have seven chapters to guide you through this.

To get an invite to interview you will already have produced a great CV or application form. The preparation that you need to do is to both re-read what you have already written and to think of examples you can use to answer questions and to practise them.

Nika, who at 18 years old has already had a number of part-time jobs and now has her first full time job, gaining every job she has ever gone for, says that the best way to get a job is to:

- smile
- be confident
- be enthusiastic
- know why you want the job.

The people you will meet

You will expect to meet the person who will interview you, but you will meet other people as well.

- **The receptionist or an administrator** who you will meet on arrival, check who you are there to see and take you to meet the interviewer.

- **One or more interviewers** who will ask you questions. These could be your potential line manager or the human resources manager.
- You may also meet **other people who you may be working** with.

You may find yourself facing more than one interview. There is sometimes an introductory first interview and then a much more detailed second interview with the best two or three candidates. The interviewers will vary from the highly trained who will ask well prepared and searching questions to those that are not prepared and could spend more time talking to you than listening and be unfocused in what they ask.

TIP

In some small companies it may not feel like an interview at all, just a chat to let them get a feel for if you would get on, so you need to expect the unexpected!

In some companies, with a close knit team you may get to meet everyone you will work with, although not all in the formal situation of the interview. When I used to manage a team we would invite short-listed candidates to meet two or three members of the team informally for a coffee to enable them to ask questions about what it was like working in our team. Before I made a final decision I would always talk with my team.

TIP

Some companies will ask the opinion of the people you meet, such as the receptionist. That's why you need to make a good impression with everyone you meet.

When you arrive

You will want to be confident when you arrive for your interview, but most of us will also feel nervous. We're concerned to do our best and often aren't really sure how the meeting will go. When we get nervous we will often breathe shallower and start to feel a bit agitated and perhaps get a knot in our stomach and even feel a bit sick.

So recognise that you might feel like this. It's a natural thing to feel and the other candidates probably feel the same. Remember to concentrate on your breathing to help you relax more.

Sometimes we feel nervous as we think we are going to be late, so make sure you have allowed plenty of time to get there. This will give you time to go to the toilet and you can wash your hands and check your hair is tidy and your tie, collar etc is straight.

POSITIVE SELF TALK

As you get close to the building remind yourself how well prepared you are. You will have read this book which will help you. Remind yourself that you are going to be great in this job. If they don't think you can do the job you wouldn't have been short-listed to interview.

You are likely to need to speak to a receptionist at an office or to a member of staff in a shop, bar, nursery etc. You need to appear confident, polite and friendly.

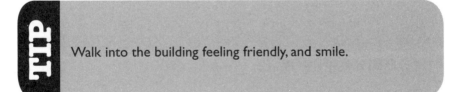

TIP

Walk into the building feeling friendly, and smile.

You'll meet with someone who will ask you a question. Listen to what they say; they'll want to know how they can help you. You will reply with something like

'I'm here for an interview – my name is Tom Smith and I have an appointment with Mr Jones at 3pm.'

Say this in a clear and confident voice tone, and try not to mumble. This is certainly something you can practise in advance. Smile as you talk and act friendly. In some companies, people you meet will be asked for their informal views on you so give them lots of positive examples to refer to.

ACTION

Say out loud what you will say to the person you will meet when you arrive for your interview. Practise until it becomes easy.

Say it out loud now, and say it a few times as you go for the interview, it will get your vocal chords warmed up and mean you don't get a dry mouth where no words come out as you try to answer a question.

You'll probably be asked to take a seat while you wait for the interview.

The interviewer will both collect you and take you to the interview room or perhaps their assistant will take you to the room. Make sure to be warm and friendly, say hello, and have a firm handshake if they offer their hand to you, but best not to put your hand out first. Sometimes an interview will involve more than one person either because there is someone there to listen in or because two (or more) people will be asking you questions. You don't always know in advance that there will be more than one person so don't let this put you off.

First impressions

People do make instant impressions on others, and so the first few minutes of an interview are vital. You need to think about how you present yourself, so act in a confident, but not cocky manner.

Remember: You only have one chance to make a first impression so make it a good one.

Many interviewers make up their minds about a candidate within seconds of meeting them. This is called the 'halo effect'. When we observe one good thing about someone, we assume all kinds of other good things about the person. It's not fair, but it's what people do.

For example, if you are well dressed, many interviewers will assume you are probably responsible in other ways, even if in truth, you are a bit scatty. This means that for everything you do right, many more good things are assumed!

Of course there is also the other side, which is called the 'horns effect'. If there is a poor first impression, you are late, mumble, or are dressed a bit scruffy then it will be very hard to correct this impression.

When you go into the interview room, wait to be asked to sit down, and think positive thoughts. If you think you will do well, you probably will, but if you think you are going to mess up the questions, then that's what will probably happen. The interview is your chance to show the interviewer that you are the person they are looking for.

Sit well back in your chair, in an upright but comfortable position. If you use your hands when talking be aware of it and don't overdo it. Make friendly eye contact with the person asking questions, but don't stare.

2

What will I be asked?

This book is all about winning interview answers, and you will see in the next five chapters that we go into significant detail on the different types of questions you may be asked alongside some example answers. These are not model answers and there are plenty of other ways to respond, but sometimes people aren't sure what to say and reading through what other people have said can spur us on to think of an example of our own.

These answers have all been used by young people I have worked with. You will read quite a bit about Tom and Kate. These are the most recent younger clients I have coached into being successful at interview and both got the jobs they wanted.

There are many different types of interview questions that you might be asked, and different ways of asking them. By the end of this chapter you will be clear on:

- the order of questions
- the different types of questions
- the style of questions
- preparing yourself.

> **TIP**
>
> You must not memorise other people's answers — your answers must be real to you, otherwise an interviewer will pick up on this and you won't get the job.

The order of questions

There is a structure to the interview and the questions you will be asked.

- Introductory questions to put you at ease.
- Questions which relate to the job and any relevant work experience you may have.
- Questions about you as a person including hobbies and interests, strengths and weaknesses.
- Time at the end for you to ask questions.

In a 30 minute interview just a couple of minutes will be spent on introductory type questions and at most 5 minutes left for the end, so you will have around 25 minutes to answer the questions asked.

 Make good use of the time – prepare strong answers to probable questions

The different types of questions

Have you ever thought about how questions can be asked in different ways? Different styles of questions can encourage you to respond very succinctly if they just want a yes or no answer or in more detail when they want you to talk.

Open questions

These are questions which cannot be answered with a yes or no answer, and are designed to get you to talk. The questions start with phrases such as:

- tell me about …
- how do you feel about …?
- describe how you …
- what sort of things have you found useful in that situation?

Probing questions

These are direct questions when the interviewer wants some specific information. They may also be used to get you to focus on a topic if you are talking too much. They are likely to be quite specific, and are similar to those listed here.

- What was your reason for …?
- Who else was involved in that project?
- How did you react to …?
- How did that affect the outcome of …?

Hypothetical questions

These questions try to place you in a 'What if' situation to see how you will respond. If you don't have experience of a work area you may be asked how you think you would deal with a particular situation. This includes questions such as:

- what would you do if an irate customer confronted you?
- tell me how you would set about organising …

Multiple questions

These questions can be confusing. Which bit do you tackle first? These may be the sign of a poorly trained interviewer, or of a memory test! Don't be fazed by it – and if you can't remember everything they asked, ask them to repeat the rest of the question. It could be a question such as:

- Can you tell me about your early school days, what you do outside work and which parts of the job you find the most frustrating?

Leading questions

Occasionally you can be asked a question where it looks like the interviewer wants you to agree with them. Sometimes it can be really sneaky and they are seeing if you will stand up to them. You must decide for yourself whether you agree or disagree with something.

- I think … What do you think?
- Isn't it quite dreadful, the way that … nowadays?

- I suppose you feel that ... is acceptable?
- I wouldn't want to try ..., would you?
- You can work under pressure can't you?

Closed questions

These questions are framed in such a way that theoretically you can answer with a yes or no. Unless it is very specific, such as 'Do you have GCSE in maths,' do go beyond the question asked to give them some more information. The questions will begin with phrases such as:

- I see you have ...
- did you like ...?
- did you feel that ...?
- have your frequent changes been due to ...?

YES OR NO QUESTIONS

Unless you are being asked something very specific, if you are asked a question that could be answered with just one word, treat it as an open question and provide a lot more detail. Let's look at some questions which fall into this category.

We want someone reliable, enthusiastic and hard working; do you tick all the boxes?
You don't give a yes or no answer but you give an example of this. Perhaps you were reliable for your paper round, enthusiastic for your studies and willing to work hard. Make sure to provide some detail.

Can you be flexible?
Again it is not yes/no but you will include an example of when you have been flexible, such as: 'Yes, I am definitely flexible, for example ...'

Do you handle conflict well?
'Yes, I do for example ...'

Do you handle pressure well?
'Yes, I do for example …'

Do you always meet deadlines?
'Most of the time. If I'm honest I did struggle when I first started studying for my A levels, but after getting a detention for handing in a piece of work late I knew I had to make sure to submit homework on time after that.'

The style of questions

Questions can be asked in either a formal or informal way, so be ready for either.

The formal style will be with questions asked in a direct style, with the interviewer or interviewers sat behind a desk and you on a straight chair in front of the interviewer(s). Questions will have been prepared and asked of each candidate and your answers noted. You may find there is little encouraging eye contact from this sort of interviewer.

The more informal style will often have you sat on an easy chair and probably with your chair at right angles to one interviewer or around a coffee table when there is more than one person. Questions will be asked less formally, but will often be searching. This is how I interview and I find that the more relaxed I make the candidates I interview, the more open they are in their responses. I always want to bring out the best from a candidate but then make very objective decisions.

IT MIGHT BE MORE THAN QUESTIONS

You may find that the interview is more than just an interview – it could be that you also have to take part in a group exercise or make a presentation, a task based exercise or perhaps they want to see how you are likely to do in the job by asking you to, for example, work on the shop floor for 30 minutes. We will cover this in Chapter 6 – Task based questions.

Preparing yourself

The general areas you need to prepare is to be able to answer the three questions.

1 What do you know about the company?
2 Why do you want to work for us?
3 How do your education, skills and experience make you suitable for this job?

You can't afford to wing it, hoping that what you say will be good enough. Don't fall into the group of people who fail to prepare – if you want this job you must be as well prepared as you possibly can be.

You can anticipate many of the questions and this book will help you to prepare for them. Questions will relate to your application form and/or CV so make sure that you can remember what you have written and can think of examples.

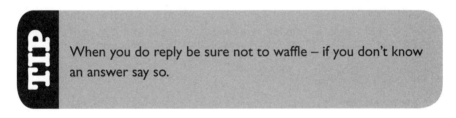

TIP When you do reply be sure not to waffle – if you don't know an answer say so.

3

Introductory questions

This chapter takes you through the very start of the interview. We'll talk about what happens in the first 5 minutes of the interview. These questions are partly about putting you at ease, but also about finding out some information to reinforce what they have read about you from your CV and/or application form.

The first few minutes of an interview are very important – they give an immediate impression to the interviewer of you. This should be positive and make the interviewer interested in finding out more about you. In this chapter we will cover:

- opening questions
- who you are.

When you go into the interview room, wait to be asked to sit down, and think positive thoughts. Remember what we said in Chapter 1? If you think you will do well, you probably will, but if you think you are going to mess up the questions, then that's what will probably happen. The interview is your chance to show the interviewer that you are the person they are looking for.

> **TIP**
>
> Some people think that the first questions don't matter; they are just a couple of questions before the interview starts proper. Don't fall into this trap! You need to be on your very best behaviour and think carefully how you answer questions right from the start.

Opening questions

They will probably ask 'How are you?' when they meet you. You might be tempted to tell them how you are really feeling and say something like:

> 'I'm really nervous; I haven't had an interview before.'

But keep these thoughts to yourself and just say something like *'I'm fine thanks'*, and smile!

Listen closely as the interviewer(s) introduces themself. You will probably want to address them by their name at some point during the interview.

How was the journey?
Sounds such a simple question doesn't it?

Peter had expected his mum to be able to drive him to the interview but on the day found out she had an important business meeting. He knew he could get a bus into town, but hadn't thought about how to get to the office which was a 15 minute walk from a bus stop. He then had to find the right building on the business park so it was all a bit of a rush. He did get there on time, just.

So when asked the question Peter said:

> 'A bit of a mare really, no idea how far out of town this building was, still I got here just on time.'

You are not talking with your friends so don't use slang such as 'mare' (short for nightmare). Also, don't be so open about your lack of preparation. The interview is meant to be important to you, so why hadn't you found out where you are going in advance?

Nadeem was also more truthful than he needed to be

> 'It was ok, but took ages, I missed the connecting bus as the train was late, and I hadn't realised I would have to leave the house so early.'

This was for a 10a.m. interview, so if he thought it was early to leave for an appointment at this time, what will it be like when he has to be in work for 8.30?

So you found the office ok?

You may not have had a problem with the journey, but maybe you did find it hard to find the building. You thought you knew where the road was, but you were mistaken and got a bit lost. Perhaps you had cycled around the business park looking for the right building. Some of these parks can have a large number of buildings and they aren't always clearly signposted.

Other times the office may be in a town centre but if you drive you may find it difficult to find the right road and even a Sat Nav doesn't help. I once drove to a meeting and the building was on the ring road in Stourbridge – it took three circuits to find the building and then another one to find out where to park. I was late and it didn't create a good impression.

You can make sure you know where you are going by downloading directions from the company web site, or asking for directions to be emailed to you. If you aren't sure where to go it's always worth doing a trial run.

These types of questions about the journey are partly to break the ice, but also to find out some very useful information. If you say how you had to take two buses, or talk about the problem with finding somewhere to park, or anything else that sounds negative, the interviewer is going to see you as someone who is likely to be late. Good time keeping is very important, so if you say things that make them wonder if you will get into work on time they are unlikely to give you the job.

Employers want staff to be punctual so make sure you are at the interview on time and keep any problems to yourself.

Good answers

How was the journey?

'The journey was great thanks, no problem at all.'

You can later decide if the journey is acceptable. You may find that it will be taking you up to 2 hours each way for travel and the travel costs are much higher than expected, in which case you will turn the job down, but it's still nice to have been offered the job.

Did you find the office ok?

'Yes thank you, your instructions were very clear.'

Would you like a drink?

There are arguments for and against saying yes to a drink. You may well be thirsty, and have a dry mouth so having some water can be useful to moisten your mouth, but you might be feeling nervous and your hand make shake a bit in which case your nerves will show to others as you either reach to take a cup and saucer or pour out some water. You need to decide what is best for you.

Who you are

Almost every interviewer I know asks this next question – '**Tell me a bit about you,**' or 'talk me through your education and work history to date'. This question is meant to put you at ease, but when I help my clients to prepare they find it anything but an easy question to answer.

There are different reasons for asking this question – partly to put you at ease by getting you to talk about the subject you know best, you! But also it's a reminder of who the interviewer has in front of them. While most interviewers will have carefully read your application form or CV and covering letter they may have eight or even more people to see in one day, and this is a quick reminder of who is in front of them.

> **TIP** There are some interviewers who haven't read the candidates' details and you may find they don't give you any eye contact as you talk as they are busy scanning your CV at the same time. Don't let this put you off!

As an interviewer, all I really want is a quick run through of what a candidate sees as the key points of their life. As a younger candidate you may wonder what to say, particularly if this is a first job. You may wonder what you can say beyond something like

> 'I'm 17 years old and I have 6 GCSEs. I've just left school and am looking for my first job. I don't mind what it is really. I'd do anything.'

If they then notice that the interviewer is looking at them they may realise they should say more, but what? So they say something like:

> 'Oh, I also like playing on my computer – I love "World of Warcraft" and watching DVDs.'

Has this really helped to make the interviewer want to know more? This is a missed opportunity, so let me take you step by step through what you need to do.

Answering the question, 'Tell me a bit about you'

Very few people can deal with this type of question without taking time to prepare and practising by saying their answer out loud to a friend or family member. Even people who have had lots of interviews can find it hard to provide a really great answer. You need a succinct and concise summary of you, your experience and achievements. This should take about 30–40 seconds.

Practising how to answer this question means you have thought through the key things you want to say and can avoid the danger of producing a rambling, boring response or a reply so short you feel like you are a rabbit trapped in headlights.

ACTION

Prepare some short notes which you can then turn into sentences.
Then practise until you remember it.

Step 1

This first step is for you to provide a short summary of yourself, your education
and what you achieved at school/college/university. It may also include details
on something relevant to the job you are applying for which will differ depend-
ing on the particular job. Here are two examples of what people have said:

'I'm 18 and gained three A levels last summer.
I did well with an A in English and Bs in
Psychology and Geography but I don't think going
to university is the right step for me. I'm very
interested in retail and want to gain experience
as a sales assistant from a company with a great
reputation such as yours.'

'I recently left college with a BTEC in Multimedia
where I specialised in graphic design and
animation. While at college I was vice-captain of
the rugby team and also did some graphic design
work for the family business.'

Step 2

Generally this is where you provide details of any work experience, concentrating on achievements and skills gained. When you have only limited work
experience you can focus more on your hobbies and interests and how you
worked well with your fellow students.

'While I was at school I wanted to concentrate on
my studies and also my sporting interests – I'm
a keen swimmer and also play hockey and tennis
so this has taken up a lot of my time. However it's

given me a lot of transferable skills. For example, I collected subs and organised the fixtures for the hockey team and alongside my swimming I also helped to coach younger swimmers one evening a week. Since leaving school I've worked part-time at the village store, predominately taking deliveries out to older villagers on my bike. However, this hasn't been a full-time job.'

'I've gained some experience of graphic design work through working in the family business. I was encouraged to create posters and covers for A4 folders, and I also created some images for use on a web presentation. Everything was quite pressurised and needed doing right away. I also learnt to use my initiative and to come up with options and alternatives to what was asked for.'

Step 3

Is there something that will make you stand out from the rest? Is there anything memorable you can say – did you win a prize, appear on TV, or go on an unusual holiday? It can be hard to think of something so let's have a look at what some other people have said:

'One thing I am really proud of is the way I was chosen to appear in a CBBC TV programme – Xchange. My hobby is Civil War re-enactment and when I was 12 I was one of two children featured in the TV programme, we spent a whole day filming.'

'I've learnt a lot from playing hockey, the importance of being part of a team, how everyone is important and the need to help each other.'

'I won a prize at school as I hadn't taken a single day off sick throughout the 5 years I was there. I was the only person to achieve it that year.'

Step 4

It is important to finish with a clear ending. Too often people just drift at the end, and in that case interviewers are never certain if people have finished or are still thinking.

Try to end with a question, such as:

'Can I tell you more on any of this?'

Practise answering the question 'Tell me a bit about you' with your friends or even better with someone you know who has been successful in interviews themselves.

Let's end this chapter with the 'Tell me a bit about you' answers from Kate and Tom.

Kate has applied for a job at a nursery and says:

'I'm Kate and I'm really interested in working with small children.

When I was at school my best subjects were Art, Music, English and History. For work experience I worked at the Stepping Stones Day Nursery and everyone told me that I was very good with the children, especially the 2–4 year olds. I did arts and crafts with them.

I'm looking for my first job but I do have some work experience. I have baby sat for a number of my mum's friends and neighbours and I've also worked in the summer, selling ice cream at the local farm shop and also clearing tables at a café.

What I'm most proud of is the birthday cards I make for my friends, everyone says they are beautiful and I make ones especially for each person.

Would you like me to tell you more on anything?'

Tom has applied for a job at a bar and says:

'I'm Tom, and I'm really pleased to be here for interview. I've recently left college with a BTEC in Multimedia. I thought I wanted to work in web design but now I've completed the course I realise that I don't want an office job, I want a more active job where I can meet people.

I did well in the group work at college and I like to be friendly with people and work as part of a team. I'm also someone who notices what needs to be done and gets on and does it.

My main hobby is music and I've been going to concerts for years. The first one I went to was Live 8 in Hyde Park. I got to see Pink Floyd who my parents had followed when they were young. I loved the atmosphere and as I was only 13 I was one of the youngest people there.

Does that tell you enough about me? I'm happy to answer any other questions you may have.'

You should now be feeling much more confident about the first few minutes of the interview. Do this well and it gets the interview off to a great start.

4

Questions about the company and the job

If you are applying for a job you need to know what the company does and what interests you about working for the company. This is all about showing that you have done your research. By the end of this chapter you will be able to demonstrate you can answer questions in the areas listed below.

- Why this job? Why have you applied for this job?
- Why us? What do you know about our company?
- What interests you about the products and services?
- Why should we offer you this job?
- Your ideal job.

The introductions are over and the main part of the interview starts. Don't forget, you have done well to get short-listed and you've been invited for interview because they think you can do the job, so stay positive. Interview questions fall into different categories and in this chapter we will cover questions around what you know about the company and questions about why you are applying for the particular job.

> **TIP**
>
> Research the company – what it does and why that interests you is essential if you want to stand out from the crowd.

It's really important to do your research in advance. You can read more about this in Chapter 5, 'Optimum performance through in-depth preparation' in *Winning Interviews for First-time Job Hunters,* published by Trotman. You can use this research to help you to answer questions and also later to help you decide what questions to ask.

I've spoken to a number of companies that take on first-time job hunters and this chapter will cover typical questions. You can also read the answers that Kate and Tom have used. They didn't always produce great answers first of all, we took the time to practise and improve on what they had to say. You can now use their answers to help you come up with something similar but which is relevant to you; you can't just say what someone else has used as you need to have the detail to expand on what you have said, should you be asked a subsequent question.

TIP

Listen carefully to the question. Sometimes questions are asked in a slightly different way, and you need to respond to the question asked.

Why this job?

Why have you applied for this job?
Why do you want this job?

I've given you the question worded in slightly different ways as I don't want you to be thrown when you don't get a question worded exactly as you see here.

These are really important questions and your answer can have a big impact on the rest of the interview. If you are unclear or vague it doesn't give a positive impression.

Interviewers want to know why you want the job, it can't be just because you haven't got one and any job would do. Well, that could be what you say, but that's not going to get you a job offer!

Your response will be based on what you have learnt about the company through your research. You will want to explain what you have found out and why it interests you. Perhaps you would like to include something about the company's reputation, or to say that you like the way the company focuses on environmental change as this is a topic you are passionate about.

Before the interview

You need to have thought through why you want the job and what you can offer to the company. You probably did this when you prepared your application, now you need to be ready to go into even more detail at the interview. This will create a great impression as you are talking from the heart rather than just giving the interviewer what you think they want to hear.

Look at two different replies from Tom,

> 'I have just left college after doing a multimedia course and I really want to get a job in graphic design.'

> 'I want to work in graphic design as I enjoy drawing, layout and design. This was my best subject at college and I have since done some work experience with family and friends to help me develop the skills of design with a client. There's nothing I want to do more in life than to work in graphic design. I particularly want to work with Tiger Design because ...'

The first reply is far too brief and hasn't sold Tom at all. The second is a more detailed reply and he is about to start talking about why he wants to work with the particular company.

TIP

There's no problem at all with anticipating a question and running that detail alongside a first question and it does help to show your enthusiasm.

Kate is applying for nursery jobs, so a different type of response is needed.

> 'I've applied for the job because I think I could bring a lot to your nursery. I've always loved working with children and I'm highly trustworthy with an outgoing personality. Through my babysitting work and part-time work at the school I've shown that I'm someone who has the ability to communicate with a wide range of children.'

Why us?

What do you know about our company?
What do you know about us?

If you are interested in retail, there are many stores out there – from food to fashion, books to jewellery, big chains to independent stores, so again think about what you will say. What would you say for example, when applying to a large national chain of opticians, what would you say differently to an independent optician?

Questions about what you know about a company are very common. Employers want applicants who have had the initiative, courtesy and enthusiasm to find out something about the organisation they are applying for. When I talk to employers they tell me this is an area that often lets candidates down; too many candidates don't show any real interest in a company and then wonder why they don't get the job. You must be able to answer this question.

What you know is not as important as that you know something! You can refer to the web site and refer to a new contract won or some community involvement, new products introduced or local competition.

TIP

Companies expect you to have done your research, so make sure you can explain what you know and why it interests you.

Again let's look at two different replies. This first one looks like it might be a good answer, but it's not addressing the question. How much detail is included on what the candidate has found out about the company?

'I'm interested in graphic design and I researched your company and thought it would be an ideal place to start. For the past few weeks I have been researching graphic design companies in this area. I know you work with Photoshop which I'm qualified in.'

A much stronger reply would be:

'As soon as I knew I had passed my course I started researching all the graphic design companies within travelling distance of my home – there's quite a few! So I set about doing research on the net and your company really stood out. I like the way that you offer a range of services and are very customer focused, you have worked with many local companies and aim to be the first choice within the local area but also do work with customers from much further away. You make great use of new technologies and also want to be seen as a great local company, taking on some charity work at a much reduced fee.'

You've already thought of a reply as to why the particular store, office etc, but what about the follow on question? You know why you want to be there, but why should they want to employ you? You might be asked questions such as: 'Why do you want to be a …?'; or, 'What do you think it takes to be successful in this job?'; or, 'Why do you think you will do well in this job?' We'll be covering these shortly.

What interests you about the products and services?

Let's assume you are applying for a retail job. There are so many shops so why are you applying for this one? The store manager/personnel manager wants to know why you want to work at their particular store, so you will avoid answers like this which are too general.

> 'I'm interested in getting a job in a shop as I like working with the public, and I think I would work well here.'

A much better reply would be

> 'I'm very interested in fashion and read fashion magazines so I know what the current trends are, but I also like to customise them. What I like about your store is that there is a quirkiness to the clothes and the way the clothes are displayed would encourage people to try out a new look. As you can see I buy my clothes from your store and I'm so excited that I might get to work here!'

Why should we offer you this job? Why does this job interest you?

You should already be clear on why this job interests you, as you would have thought about this as you put your application together. Now the interviewer wants to hear *in your own words*. They know that sometimes people have

TIP

You must talk about what you can offer the company, not the benefits to you. Don't talk about the salary or perks, or that it's close to where you live. You need to think about what an employer wants to hear.

had help with their application forms, CV and covering letter, so asking the question will allow them to see if you can remember what you wrote, but also so they can follow up with a secondary question, which they are very likely to.

The importance of preparation

As part of your preparation you should have been finding out about the company so now is your chance to demonstrate what you have found out. You need to refer to what you have read in their brochures, which is usually available as a download from their web site and also anything you have read about them through news sites. Perhaps they have won a new order or introduced a new product. Some of the employees may have done some charity work. They may be a US subsidiary or be the head office for a worldwide company. Is this something that interests you? Why? Be ready to ask a question, but also know why you are asking it.

You may have found out loads, but you aren't writing an essay or giving a 20 minute presentation so you need to think about how you can clearly describe what you found out. Think about what are the key points you want to say – something about the history, successes, current challenges, and something that you had to dig deeper for, not obvious from the web site.

ACTION

Write down your notes and read them aloud. Then put your notes to one side and see how much you can remember.

Outline how well you match up to the job. Emphasise what you can contribute, rather than what you can take. For example, if you want a job in a high street fashion store you could say:

> 'This job is a perfect match for my skills and aspirations. I love working with people and I love

fashion. I can't think of anything better than working in your shop. I know that working in a shop is a hard job, but I'm used to standing on my feet each day and I'm also keen to help out, I don't mind having to vacuum or dust.'

TIP

The interviewer wants you to show enthusiasm and passion. So don't just go through the motions, let them know how enthusiastic you are!

Natalie has applied for a job as a customer service assistant and says:

'XYZ are noted for their high standard of customer care and are well respected in the community. I want to use my knowledge of customer service in a company I can be proud to work for. I've heard that people are well treated, get excellent training and vacancies rarely come up. You'll have had a lot of applications but I think my interest in helping people and my ability to speak clearly will be a real asset to your company.'

The follow up question could be asking you more about how you can relate your background to the job – 'What do you think you could bring to the company?'

This is where you relate your particular skills, knowledge and experience against the requirements of the job. So you must re-read your application so you can quickly summarise what you included in your covering letter.

Why do you want to be a ...?

Companies want to know what interests you about a profession or job. Too often people give a bland reply as they haven't really given this any thought and they don't care whether they get this job or another one. But the interviewer cares, and they want to know why you want this job.

I'm going to focus on two specific jobs – graphic design and customer service to show you how to answer these questions.

> **TIP**
>
> Every job and profession has a unique element, and so you should tailor your response to what is key about a role. For a nurse it could be to do with helping people, and for sales it could be competition and money.

When Tom was asked 'Why do you want to work as a graphic designer?', he said:

> 'Firstly, it's what I've been studying for and I've already learnt how to use Photoshop, 3D Studio, Flash and Illustrator. I'm very good with IT and have some knowledge of Dreamweaver for web design.
>
> I'm also highly creative and love coming up with new ideas. With the design work I've been doing for the family business I've been learning to listen to what other people want rather than giving people what I think they want. What I'm really interested in is helping a company be more effective and to get more business through its use of layout and design. Working as an intern has been really helpful as I've been along to client meetings and got to learn about how their business has improved following the work we have done, that's really interesting and helps me understand how the graphic design work helps business! Graphic design is my passion – it's the job I've got to do, and I know I have lots still to learn but I'm a quick learner and very keen to learn and take account of feedback.'

This is a good answer, and his enthusiasm and passion is clear. What he said was partly based on what he knows about graphic design through his research, but also relating it to what he had done.

They could then ask a follow-up question – 'What are the qualities needed to be an effective ...?'

Think of a job that you are interested in. Make a note of some of the skills and personal characteristics that are needed. You may have found these via the job advertisement or information provided. If not you can find out more by doing some research on the Internet. Look on web sites such as

http://careersadvice.direct.gov.uk/helpwithyourcareer/jobprofiles/

Read carefully about the skills and knowledge needed for the particular job. You can then use this as your start and provide specific examples.

For example if you want to be a customer service assistant, using the web link above you can find that the skills and knowledge needed are:

- a genuine interest in helping customers
- excellent communication skills
- the ability to work as part of a team
- a polite, tactful and friendly attitude
- patience and calmness under pressure
- the ability to handle complaints and difficult situations
- computer and administrative skills
- basic mathematical skills.

You probably wouldn't want to refer to all of these but pick out the top four or five and use this as your answer alongside some specific examples of your experience.

ACTION

Think of a job which interests you, do some research and make a note of the key skills and knowledge needed.

Natalie is interested in a job in customer service. She would say something like:

> 'I'm very interested in work as a customer service assistant and believe that to be effective in this job the most important qualities are to *enjoy working with people* and to want to help them. I've met some difficult people through some voluntary work in a cha rity shop and I learnt that you *need to stay calm* and let the person know you are listening to them. It's also important to *work well as part of a team* and to help each other out as necessary. To keep the admin straight a customer service assistant would need *good computer and filing skills* and I do have a great *attention to detail*. I'm known for being accurate and when working at the nail salon I would do a lot of the office work. I'm *good with numbers* as well and got a grade A in my GCSE Maths.'

As you can see Natalie gave quite a comprehensive reply, taking account of the skills and knowledge that are needed, and weaving in some of her strengths as well. As you can see above I've highlighted in bold the points that relate to the skills and knowledge identified as needed in the job.

Sometimes we are applying for a job for work experience, perhaps as part of a gap year between A levels and university. For some jobs companies will prefer people who will stay for longer, you should probably be open that you will be leaving for university but emphasise your strengths, particularly about being quick to learn and anything else which is key to the job.

Rachael was very keen to get a job in telephone sales prior to going to university as she could see a lot of benefits to a future career. It would help:

- enhance her communication skills
- develop the skills of persuasion
- help her to deal with rejection.

She knew this is a feature of many jobs when you need to persuade others and she wanted to learn how to deal with this early on in her career.

Your ideal job

Sometimes you may be asked about your ideal job, with questions such as 'If you could choose any job what would it be?', 'What is your dream job?' or 'What is your ideal job?'

This is not the time to say how you have always wanted to be a rock star, or to be PA to a famous footballer. It's unlikely that your dream job is to work in a shop, or be a trainee mechanic but the interviewer wants to hear that you are interested in this job so it would be better to say something like

> 'I'm looking for a job where I can work with people in a busy working environment and where there's room to develop. This job lets me do all three.'

Are you applying for other jobs?

Sometimes you will be asked outright if you are applying for other jobs. Of course you will be, no one is going to apply for just one job at a time and if another company is interested in you it does make you appear more attractive.

You want to come across as someone who has been short-listed by other companies so the interviewer thinks you are wanted by other companies as well, but you also need to reinforce your interest in the job. You could easily find yourself giving more detail than you need to, so a good response could be something like:

> 'I really want this job with you, but I can't assume that I'll get this so yes I am applying for other jobs, but this is the one I want.'

5

Competency questions (about your experience and skills)

This chapter will focus on competency based questions. By the end of this chapter you will be clear on the following.

- What are competency based questions?
- The need for specific rather than general examples.
- Why you should use the STAR approach.
- How to prepare for competency based questions.
- How to answer competency based questions.

What are competency based questions?

This is a particular type of question where you need to provide a specific example. The questions are based on competences which have been identified by the company through job analysis. This is where the company identifies what is of key importance to a job such as relationships with people, communication, problem solving and creative thinking.

With a competency based question you can choose examples from any aspect of your life, so don't feel you have to focus purely on work experience. The question does get you to focus on an actual example, so don't talk in broad terms but describe one particular situation.

> **TIP**
>
> You will be asked for specific examples, so think about what you have done – from studies, hobbies and any part-time work that you can discuss.

You can sometimes identify if competency based questions will be used through the details of a job. For example, if you applied for a job with the Department for Work and Pensions (DWP) as an administrator, the competences listed are:

- engaging effectively with customers
- improving performance
- making best use of resources
- building constructive working relationships.

The application form will have asked you to choose how you would respond to various situations. You will then be asked for more detailed examples against these competencies at interview.

When you apply for some jobs it may not always be obvious that you will be assessed against competencies but there are **clues in the questions asked**. We'll be looking at a range of questions and looking at example answers, so you will be more confident when you are asked competency based questions.

The need for specific rather than general examples

For competency based questions it is very important that you can provide a specific example. Too often as an interviewer I find that people give very vague replies. They talk in general terms rather than thinking of a particular situation. When I talk to other interviewers they say the same: while a specific question is asked, a woolly, generalised reply is usually received. This happens in all sorts of competency based interviews, with all sorts of people, not just with younger candidates. A generalised reply is not helpful and won't get you good marks in the interview. **You need to give a specific example to the specific question.**

Let's have a look at some of the questions you could be asked and we'll then move on to how to answer these competency based questions in three areas.

Personal questions such as:

- tell me about an achievement you are proud of?
- give me an example of when your work has been criticised. How did you respond?

People questions such as:

- tell me how you have established a good working relationship with new people?
- tell me about a time when you helped resolve a dispute between others?

Work situation questions such as:

- please provide an example of where you have had to provide a product or service to a customer?
- tell me about a mistake and what you have learnt from this?

Why you should use the STAR approach

There's a straightforward approach which should be helpful. It's called the STAR approach. Following this structure helps you to provide a specific example – so you give the interviewer what they are looking for, and you stand a better chance of doing well.

ANSWER QUESTIONS USING
THE STAR APPROACH

Most questions ask about your past or current experience from work study or leisure activities. When talking about these subjects, choose specific examples to illustrate your answer. Describe the **Situation** you were in, the **Task** you were asked to accomplish, the **Action** you took and why, and the **Results** of your actions. This will help the interviewer follow your 'story' and see your accomplishments.

Here's an example of a response that uses this method to address an interviewer's question.

Situation:
I didn't handle the transition to college well and failed my first year exams.

Task:
I knew that if I wanted to succeed, I had to develop better study habits and manage my time better.

Action:
I created a calendar and marked the due dates for all of my assignments and tests. Then I set aside certain hours each day for studying, allowing more for the exam times.

Result:
My essays were in on time, and I took notes regularly to make things easier for exams. Because I was separating study time from social time, I would work hard and then relax, which has helped my time management.

Be prepared to answer some follow up questions, you don't just answer a question and sit back, there will be follow up questions as well so the interviewer really understands what you are saying. The interviewer may want to get some more specific detail on what you were thinking or what happened when you spoke to the person you mentioned so you need to be very clear on your example, you can't make one up!

How to prepare for competency based questions

You can get prepared for competency based questions by thinking of examples from your life. If you have already had some work experience you can choose work based examples, but you can also use examples from your studies, hobbies, other interests and perhaps some voluntary work.

Your examples will certainly include times when things have gone well and you achieved something, but you can also have examples of times when you may have struggled, things haven't gone as easily, but you made the best of a situation or where you got a positive outcome in the end.

It's going to be helpful to prepare so let's get you thinking about some specific area you may be asked questions on.

ACTION

Consider carefully how you could answer questions on the areas detailed below. Write down your examples in the space provided.

Personal questions

Let's start by thinking of **examples of when you have achieved something**, perhaps passing exams, winning an award, learning to do something? Make a note of things you have done in the space below. You can later come back and think about which is your best example.

In the workplace you often have **more than one task to do at once** – it is called multi tasking. You probably had to do this when you were studying, especially at exam time or perhaps it was combining study with your role in the school play? Can you think of a time when you had a lot on? Make a note here.

Sometimes we find that **we are criticised**. Most of the time this is because of something we did or didn't do. I'm sure you can think of a time when this happened to you, could you make a note of something here?

Employers also want to know about **goals you have set for yourself**. This could be to learn something new, and you might be able to use this to answer the achievement question above, but it could be a separate one so see what you can think of and make a note here.

TIP Remember, the answers must refer to a specific example and not be vague!

People questions

Employers want to know how you will **get on with other people**, which could include colleagues and customers/clients. It might also include how you get on with bosses or teachers or your involvement with sports teams. So have a think about the people you have worked with and make a note of times when you have worked really well with others. Also think about any examples you have when it didn't go as easy. Make a note overleaf.

Working with people can also include **helping to keep the peace** or intervening in a dispute. Can you think of a time you have done something like this? If you can, make a note below.

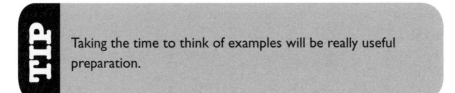

TIP

Taking the time to think of examples will be really useful preparation.

Work situations

You will be asked questions about relevant work experience to see how well you can see yourself matching up to the job. You can't just say that you don't have any experience so think about anything that has a connection to the job.

Work experience is much broader than a full-time job. It can also include Saturday jobs, holiday jobs and also work experience gained while at school.

If you don't have any work experience, the interviewer will know this and so won't ask you questions which specifically focus on work. However there are questions that relate to work, in the sense of achieving a task, and these are included here. You also need to think more broadly and look to examples in all areas of your life, including school and hobbies.

Kate was asked about relevant experience to the job of nursery nurse. She hadn't had a paid job but had done some baby sitting so was able to use that as an example. She could also discuss playing with some of her young cousins.

Employers are going to be interested in times when you have **worked with customers**. If you haven't had a job yet what else could be relevant? Your 2 week work experience could be used here. Or perhaps you could talk about a group project. Can you write down an example below?

We sometimes have **problems in our work** due to faulty equipment, not getting the stock in that a client wants etc. There may also be a problem you could use to do with your studies such as finding it difficult to get relevant items for a project. So think about what you could say and make a note below.

When employers ask you a question about **mistakes you have made**, your answer could be from any area of your life. Things do go wrong but then we learn from them, so make a note of when something has gone wrong and what you learnt from it.

Sometimes we need to **make a decision when we don't have all the information we need**. Can you think of a situation? If so, make a note below.

Then there are the **stressful situations**. Once you start work it could be stressful because of some of the people you have to work with or the range or pace of tasks that need completing. They want to know that you have experience of dealing with difficult or stressful situations, so can you think of an example?

Finally let us think of times when you have **shown some initiative**. There are likely to be times when you were left to do something without having someone to ask, or a time where you noticed something and got on with it. If you can think of an example, make a note below.

Team working

Most jobs involve working as part of a team, but not all jobs. So think through, would you prefer to work alone or as part of a team? You may be asked this question

Tell me about a time when you have worked in a team
You need to think of an example or two of what teams you have been involved in, so get prepared now. Rather than move on, make a note below.

How are you at working alone?
Some jobs do involve you working alone and so you might be asked this question. We have all worked alone when we have revised so you could say use that as an example or something else.

What's the greatest team you have ever been involved in and why?
It's one of those questions where you need to have thought about the experiences you have had to be able to think on your feet.

Tell me when you needed to put your own needs to one side to help someone else
Have you ever done this? Helping someone out in one situation can mean that an interviewer will believe you will be able to do this in the future. Can you think of an example? If so, make a note here.

It's easy to just skim over an exercise like this and ignore it, but that's unlikely to help you with a forthcoming interview; doing these exercises is very good preparation.

How to answer competency based questions

Let's now look at how you can answer these questions, and a few others!

We'll use the three categories we have looked at earlier and use the same questions you have already thought about. If you didn't come up with examples relevant to you, go back and make a note now.

Personal questions

Tell me about an achievement you are proud of
Achievements don't have to be over-the-top examples where you were the absolute winner; they could also be a time when you did something that was difficult for you, such as learning to swim or passing an exam in your weakest subject. Or perhaps it could be about you taking part in a school play when

you are really shy. So think about examples from your studies, sports and any other areas that might be relevant.

'I am very proud of the way I got into the school football team. I had to practise really hard so it was such great news when I made the team.'

'I know how important it is to do well in maths and worked really hard to make sure I got a good grade. Maths has never been my best subject and I was really pleased to get a grade C I, it really was an achievement.'

'I'm quite shy and make a real conscious effort to talk to people. I've found that working at the café on a Saturday helped as I had to talk with the customers and I've now got much better at talking to new people.'

If you answer in a more vague way such as *'Getting 7 GCSEs at A–C, I'm proud of that,'* the interviewer is likely to ask some follow up questions such as: 'Why does that make you proud?' So you must think of why you feel proud, and one way of replying could be something like:

'Because I had struggled, especially with science and maths and, if I'm honest I didn't work as hard as I could, so in my second year I really worked hard, and also made sure that if I wasn't clear on anything I asked, rather than not saying anything which is what I had done in the past.'

Tell me about a time you have had multiple priorities
How did you ensure the work got done?
This question is asking about the way you plan and prioritise your time. While you want to be seen as someone who is flexible and doesn't need to stick to set hours, you will also want to show how you will manage your time by differentiating between what is important and urgent. Here are a couple of answers which might give you an idea on what to say.

'Probably studying for my A levels was the hardest, I had so much revision to do and some days I had two exams on the same day. I created a plan and stuck it on a wall so I could refer to it.'

'There was a lot of work to do when studying for my BTEC, as I was studying for different subjects, plus I had some gigs with the band I sing with. I knew I wanted to do well, and I knew there were going to be times, like at exams with lots to do, so I made a clear revision plan and made sure that everything would get done, and it was!'

Give me an example of when your work has been criticised How did you respond?

The best way to reply to this is to talk about an idea of yours that was criticised, not your work. If you have some work experience you don't want to talk about being criticised for timekeeping, the way you spoke to a customer etc, and at school or college you don't want to talk about how you were criticised because of not completing a project. Those sorts of reply will leave a negative impression with the interviewer.

It's very tempting to give an answer like: 'If my work is ever criticised I listen carefully and make sure I take account of it for next time. It can hurt me a bit as I want to do well but I know I have things to learn, and I want to do better.' But this is very vague and doesn't include anything specific. It also sounds like an answer you have learned and so not that real! The examples below are much better.

'I was involved in a meeting about fundraising for Friends of the Earth. I made some suggestions for how we could get some publicity such as abseiling down the Eagle Tower Building but no one else was interested in this and I was told that my suggestion was stupid. This hurt, and I learnt that when some people ask for suggestions they don't always want to hear things that are very different to things that have been done before.'

'I was working on a group project and we each had our own tasks to do. I had thought I understood what I needed to do but the work I brought back to the group wasn't right as I had misunderstood what I was meant to do. One of the group was quite critical and said I had let the group down. I was very hurt and felt very embarrassed. Afterwards I realised that the instructions hadn't been clear and although I had wasted some time I could still get the right work done later. I learnt that I should always summarise a task to make sure I was going to do the right thing.'

'I produced some course work and gave it to my lecturer at college for feedback. He was quite blunt in his feedback. It wasn't nice to be criticised but good to be told how to improve it before I submitted it. I thought about what he'd said and I realised that I hadn't gone into enough detail and it was helpful to be told how to improve. That made it easier for me to change what I'd written and I then got a decent mark.'

You will see that in these examples there is a final sentence which outlines what was learnt from the situation. It's likely that an interviewer will ask you what you have learnt if you don't include this. By including details on what you have learnt, without being asked, demonstrates you can be reflective.

People questions

Tell me how you have established a good working relationship with new people

You should have plenty of examples to talk about through working with other people at school or college, even if you don't have any work experience. Again you want to be specific, and an answer like 'I'm just me, I'm outgoing and friendly with people and people seem to like me,' lacks the detail included in the examples below.

'A good example would be when I moved from school to college, none of my friends made the move and so I needed to be open to make friends. I made sure I was friendly with others, listened to what other people had to say and in any group work that I always did my share of the work.'

'I got some part-time work delivering groceries from the local shop to housebound villagers. I'm quite shy and at first I just handed the box of groceries over, but I soon realised that people were lonely and wanted to talk so I made sure to ask them how they were and listen to them.'

Tell me about a time when you helped resolve a dispute between others

We often find that our friends fall out and this could be a really good example to this sort of question, so a reply could be something like:

'Sometimes my friends would argue at school so I would tell them to calm down and listen to each of them. I think my friends see me as a bit of a peace maker as I can see both sides and help others do the same.'

Work situations

Please provide an example of where you have had to provide a product or service to a customer

A lot of jobs involve working with customers so it's good to have an example ready. If you don't have a work example, you could use an example from school or college such as providing some work on time, for example for an art exhibition or a school show. Let's look at some examples that might give you some ideas.

'In the café I would serve the customers who came in and would always try my best to be polite and friendly, even with those who were a bit difficult.'

'I don't have any paid work experience, but I have been doing some babysitting and I am always polite to the families whose children I look after and make sure to have some fun with the children if I am looking after them during the daytime.'

What skills have you gained from your work experience?

It's another question which asks you to be reflective. Don't worry if your work experience is not from a full-time or part-time job but from a 2 week work placement while at school. This is absolutely fine and you can use this to answer the questions above. You also want to think about what you learned from this work experience.

ACTION

Think about some work experience you have, and what you gained from it.

Not everyone has thought carefully about a particular work placement and you might have been like Tim and worked at the local garage because it was close to home, or like Susie, whose dad arranged for her to work at his office (a solicitors' office). Both Tim and Susie were not interested in this work and found it difficult to think of anything to say. But actually to learn that you are not interested in a job is also useful. So if this is you, you could say something like:

'I thought I might like office work but I didn't really enjoy it, and it made me realise that I'd rather have a job where I get out and about, that's why I'm interested in training to be an electrician.'

But you may have gained a lot from your work experience in which case you could say something like:

'Working for 2 weeks at a vet's made me much clearer that I do want to be an animal nurse. I love animals and I liked watching what the vet does. I hadn't realised what the job was all about, but after 2 weeks I know that alongside helping in the consulting rooms it is also looking after the animals that have to stay over. I was happy to do the cleaning work as well and understand that this is an important part of the job.'

Tell me about a problem you have solved

You can't say that you didn't have any problems and whatever you do say, make sure the problem was overcome. You might like to talk about a mistake and what you have learnt from it. Oliver struggled with how to answer and then thought about an example related to his passion, playing in a band.

'I play bass guitar in a band and our lead singer left suddenly so we needed to find someone to replace her as the rest of us aren't very good singers. None of us really knew what to do, so I decided to put a note to all my friends on Facebook, and for them to contact their friends. This meant we had a few people to audition.'

Tell me about a time when you have had to make a decision when you didn't have all the information you needed

'The best example was my choice of A levels, I didn't know what career I would want to pursue and knew that my choice of A levels could rule out certain university courses if I didn't take the right subjects. I spent the summer reading about different careers and then chose the subjects to study that both interested me and I was likely to get the best grades for.'

Do you think this is a good answer? Other answers could include a choice over summer work experience or in what sort of voluntary work to pursue as part of a gap year.

Can you tell me when you have had to deal with a difficult or stressful situation?

You could use your example of dealing with multiple priorities as that was likely to be stressful. Whatever example you use make sure that it is something that you can discuss in depth. For example

'After exams I travelled with three school friends to Paris so that we could visit Euro Disney. This was the first time we had been abroad alone and it was quite stressful. Once we crossed the channel we had to change trains and all the instructions were in French and no one was sure what to do. I suggested that we followed other people with luggage as I assumed there were also going to Paris, which they were.'

Tell me about a time when you have shown some initiative

The answers below focus on two quite different scenarios. Make sure that the example you choose is something you can discuss at length.

'I attended boarding school as a day girl and as I moved into 6th form decided that I wanted to board. I knew I would have to convince my parents to allow me to do this as my mother wanted me to stay at home and also there were the extra costs. I found out how much this would cost and also the house I wanted to board at. I also explained the benefits to my parents of me going away from home. As the only daughter I knew my mum would find it hard when I left for university and I hoped to go to St Andrews which was over 300 miles away from where we lived. I explained that while I would be away from home I would only be a few miles from our house and could easily meet up with my mum each week.'

'At school we are encouraged to do some voluntary work each week. Most students choose to work with older people. I decided to work at a residential school for young people with severe autism as I know that it can be very hard for them to communicate and I thought that this would help to develop my communication skills. I didn't choose the easy option, but something I could learn from. Also there was no school connection with this school and I took the initiative to get in touch and arrange this.'

Team working

Most jobs involve working as part of a team, but not all jobs. So think through, would you prefer to work alone or as part of a team? You may be asked this question.

Tell me about a time when you have worked in a team

We have all worked with others so you need to think of examples that you can discuss in more detail. Other people have said things such as:

'Playing rugby was all about being part of a team and we all had to work well together. You couldn't just do your own thing but had to think about what was going to be best for all. The practising we did helped us to understand where out strengths lay and that we had to think of others and not just what we wanted to do.'

'I spent last summer helping out at a children's summer play scheme. Five of us worked together, and I was one of the two youngest. We had to decide between us who was to do what and we needed to be able to cover for others – if one of the children got upset it might mean I would have to move on to some different work.'

How are you at working alone?

We have all worked alone when we have revised so you could say something like:

'At college I had to do a lot of study on my own and I was able to do this without any problems.'

What's the greatest team you have ever been involved in and why?
Matt was asked this when he applied for a job with a mobile phone company and he said:

'This would be my rugby team when I was at school. We had to work well together, to understand each other's strengths and to look out for each other. We socialised outside of the games as by knowing each other it helped us to work better on the pitch. This was the first time I had ever felt like I was in a great team and I'm looking forward to working as part of a team in a job.'

It's one of those questions where you need to have thought about the experiences you have had to be able to think on your feet.

Tell me when you needed to put your own needs to one side to help someone else
Not all my clients can think of an answer to this one. Andrew gave this as an example:

'I was revising for a test when a friend rang in a panic as she was really struggling with algebra, something that I knew well. I knew I would do ok so I left my revision to help her out. I still passed my test and Alex did as well. I was glad to have helped.'

6

Task based questions

An interview can sometimes be more than an interview, to include questions where you need to image yourself in a particular scenario, tasks involved in working with other candidates, and where you need to write or present. You could be asked to do things in advance, such as prepare for a presentation. At other times it will be in addition or sometimes even instead of an interview as a first stage to being selected for a job. All will be covered here. By the end of this chapter you will be clear on how to give your best during:

- situational/hypothetical questions
- group interviews
- practical exercises
- presentations
- written exercises
- research challenges
- group discussions.

Situational questions/hypothetical questions

Sometimes an interviewer will ask questions, not about your work experience, but hypothetical work situations. These questions ask how you think you would handle a particular situation.

These sorts of questions include

‘Your team leader is off sick and you have an angry customer on the phone, what would you do?’

To answer this question well you need to imagine yourself in the job. I know this can be really hard when you are asked to do this with no time to think in advance, and this is why it can be very helpful to have found out what's involved in the job you are applying for and to have talked with others who know about the job. That means you can think about this in advance.

> 'When you are greeting customers, how can you make them feel welcome and comfortable?'

We have all been in shops and cafés and so we know how we have been treated. What did you like? When did you feel welcome? You can use these experiences as examples.

> 'What three things would a customer expect from us?'

Obviously this will depend on the job. Chris was asked this when applying for a job at a garage where he would work on the till. He told me later that he had said – 'clean and friendly; gets you what you want; you don't have to queue for long'.

ACTION

Make a note of how you would answer this, especially if you are interested in a customer focused job.

Let's look at a couple of examples:

Trainee motor vehicle technician

If you are interested in becoming a motor vehicle technician, the job involves finding faults, talking with customers, estimating how much something will

TIP

Find out about the different skills needed and tasks undertaken for a particular job. This means you are able to anticipate the sorts of questions you might be asked.

cost, carrying out repairs and servicing vehicles. A hypothetical question could ask you about what you think are the key things you would need to do in the job. So if you have found out what the job involves it makes answering so much easier.

If you were applying for a job as a motor vehicle technician and you were asked the question 'What three things would a customer expect from us?', you could use this detail about the job to help you answer this question.

ACTION

How would you answer the question: 'What three things would a customer expect from us?' if you were applying for a job as a trainee motor vehicle technician?

Nursery nurse

If you are interested in becoming a nursery nurse, the job involves planning and supervising activities such as arts and crafts, helping children develop language skills and number skills, feeding and bathing babies and also being aware of health and safety. It's this final aspect that might form the basis of a hypothetical question. So you could be asked a question such as 'Working with young children means we need to pay attention to health and safety, what do you think we need to do?'

A possible reply could include:

> 'A risk assessment would identify possible problem areas such as checking the children were safe from danger – so anything that might hurt them would be kept locked away, and soft surfaces were around anywhere the children might fall and hurt themselves.'

Group interviews

Sometimes a company will have an initial group interview to help them to narrow down the people who get an individual interview. Richard told me about the way that he was recruited for one of the chains of motorway service stations. Anyone who applied could get a group interview and these were held on a weekly basis. The head of HR would give a short talk and the candidates were then split into smaller groups where, for about 30 minutes, they were asked work related questions. These were not targeted at individuals but asked to the group. If you had the confidence to speak up you were more likely to be short-listed than if you were shy and a bit hesitant.

In a group discussion, you must be ready to talk. It doesn't matter how brilliant your thoughts are if you don't say them out loud no one will know.

Practical exercises

Often an interviewer will want to see how you actually approach a task, rather than how you think you will do something. The tasks are generally quite straightforward but there can be a tendency to panic and to let go of all common sense. Relax! If you are applying for a job as a sales associate for a company, you will have already thought about what the job involves and a lot of that involves talking with customers.

If you are applying for a job in a store the work is likely to involve:

- serving and advising customers
- taking payment by cash or card
- helping customers to find the goods they want
- advising on the availability of stock
- giving information on products and prices
- promoting any special offers or store cards
- ordering goods that are unavailable
- handling any complaints or passing them on to a manager
- stacking shelves or displaying goods in an attractive way
- arranging window displays
- receiving stock.

> You can find out the detail on any job by looking up the job at
> http://careersadvice.direct.gov.uk/helpwithyourcareer/jobprofiles/

As you can see from the list on the previous page most of this involves contact with customers and so a practical exercise is likely to involve customer contact.

> Paul applied for a job as a sales assistant in a national retail store. He had expected an interview but after a short chat was taken on to the sales floor. Firstly he was asked to hand out baskets as people walked into the store, with the interviewer watching to see how he related to the customers. His second task was to hand out leaflets to customers. Paul was quite confident and chatted with customers. He was also smartly dressed and so 'looked the part'. The final part of the interview was a second short interview, and the next day he got a phone call to say he had got the job.

If you are applying for a job working in administration, using the careers advice web site again you will see that the job involves:

- dealing with incoming and outgoing post
- maintaining stationery supplies
- answering the telephone and directing calls
- reception duties such as greeting and looking after visitors
- typing and formatting documents such as letters and reports
- updating computer databases
- filing
- using office equipment such as printers, photocopiers and fax machines
- managing diaries
- making travel arrangements for staff.

Some of these tasks involve working with people but a lot is to do with being accurate.

Jaz applied for a job as an admin assistant working for part of the health service. She was told in advance that there would be a filing test. When we talked I said that based on what I had read in the job description the test was likely to be to check on accuracy, as the role involved looking after patient records. While speed was important, more than anything she should be as accurate as possible and in the interview part of the meeting to say that when she does a new task she takes great care to get it right but then does get quicker. This was exactly the exercise set and she said she didn't panic, took her time, and noticed the small errors put into the exercise — filing had to be done under the surname but a couple of the folders had been incorrectly completed with the first name first.

Presentations

A presentation can appear very scary — having to speak for 5 minutes or even longer, and in front of people you don't know. Companies use presentations to get a feel about your personality — are you outgoing, 'up for it' and also to see how you deal with a stressful situation.

The presentation can often be part of a group interview. For companies that get a lot of applications this can be a cost effective method of deciding who to take forward to a personal interview.

Rob applied for a job in a large supermarket chain as a trainee manager. The first stage of the selection was a group interview. One of the area managers spoke to the group of applicants and told them about what the job involved and how competitive the selection was. I had told him to make sure to speak up to make sure he was noticed in the first part of this interview. The second part was the individual presentations. Everyone was asked to talk for 3 minutes on a subject of their choice and had just 5 minutes to prepare.

The best preparation you can do is to be ready to talk on a subject that you know about and are passionate about. It could be to do with a hobby or interest, but make sure that when you do give the presentation it doesn't come across as over prepared. Have 3 or 4 key points that you can use. Alternatively you could choose an example which demonstrates your organisational skills or using your initiative, such as if you have organised a trip for your friends.

Written exercises

Sometimes you are asked to write something. If a job involves written work (for example if you are applying for a job in a public relations company as a PR assistant) a company will want to make sure that you can do what you say you can do. If we look at the key elements of a job in PR it includes things to do with creating good relationships with others such as clients and the media, good organisational skills to monitor press coverage and also:

- writing and editing leaflets and brochures
- producing press releases
- writing talks and speeches
- writing 'copy' for newsletters and web sites.

As you can see, writing is a key element of the job and so rather than just rely on you saying that you can write well, you could be asked to write something such as a press release.

> **TIP**
>
> The best preparation for a job which involves a significant writing element is to practise writing under time constraints.

Research challenges

If the job you are applying for involves finding things out you may find that you are given a task to do to see how well you can find out information, again under tight time constraints.

In this type of interview you will be asked to go and find something out. For example, if you are applying for a junior researcher role you may be given access to a phone and a computer and asked to find a particular expert.

If you are faced with a research task, make sure you really understand what you are meant to do. The question may be purposely confusing to check that you make sure that you fully understand the task.

Group discussion

Most companies want people who get on with each other and who can communicate well with each other. People can say that they can do this, but is this just something that candidates are saying that they can do, can they really work well with others?

There are different styles of group exercise.

- **You are given a group task which is a problem to be solved.** Often you are each given some information but nobody has all the detail, you need to share information between each other. There is one exercise which involves information on five different people, five different places where people live, five different vehicles and five different pets and as a group you need to piece together who lives next to whom.
- **You are given a practical activity.** This could be where you are asked to make something out of building bricks or a variety of small items. One task was for a group to work together and work out how over what distance they could transport an egg with the target being from one side of a table to the other.
- **You are set a scenario and you need to make a decision.** A typical discussion would be 'desert survival' and there is in-depth detail on this if you do an Internet search. The scenario is that you were all on a plane which has crashed and you have to individually put into order the items worth saving which include a mirror, which would

help you to signal for help and a tarpaulin, useful for shelter and to catch water.

- **You have to discuss information and reach a conclusion.** This could be related to the job or something in the news. Topics could include 'how to get more customers' or 'how to get media coverage' to being put in a scenario set 10 or 20 years into the future where you need to think about how you would deal with a particular situation. For example, discussing ways to reduce energy usage or discussion on how to get more young people involved in sport.

In some of these cases you would be given some reading to do at the start of the discussion.

Be involved and interested in what other people have to say; referring to people by name will help.

7

Questions about you

Interviewers are going to want to know more about you, especially when you don't have much work experience, so let's have a look at some of the questions they may ask you. Obviously I don't know exactly what you will be asked, but having spoken to a number of interviewers and my younger clients, these questions have been used several times. By the end of this chapter you will be clear on how to give your best, answering questions related to:

- hobbies and interests
- working with others
- personal qualities
- strengths and weaknesses
- questions about your education
- flexibility and ability to get to work on time
- future plans and goals.

Let's now look into more detail on questions you may be asked and how other people have replied.

Hobbies and interests

This category is straightforward, it wants to know more about what you do in your spare time and also if you can see any connection to the job you are applying for. Let's look at a couple of questions you could be asked.

What are your interests? What do you do in your spare time?

We don't just work or study, we have time to do other things, so what do you do? An interviewer wants to know more about you, and the things that interest you. It could be that you are a musician and spend a lot of time practising and playing in a band or orchestra. You may be at school or college, and outside of study you have a part-time job, so any time outside that is spent relaxing in front of the TV. What will you say that will interest an interviewer?

Interests can include things we do on our own such as reading, stamp collecting or listening to music. Others will be activities we do with others such as sports — football, hockey, dancing. Some activities are obviously relevant to a job such as if you help out at an after school club for younger children, or you are a prefect, or perhaps set up the school recycling group.

ACTION

So what about you? Make a note of your hobbies and interests.

Let's have a read of what other people have said:

> 'I enjoy fishing and whenever I have some free time I go out fishing with my friend. What I like about fishing is that it's very relaxing, but it's also being active and I enjoy being in the fresh air. I'm interested in fish and also have tropical fish at home. I've kept fish since I was 9 years old and know quite a bit about the subject. I recently had an article published in *Aquarium* magazine - not bad for a 17 year old.'

> 'I love to dance, and this takes up a lot of my spare time. I'm particularly interested in street dance but I also do tap dancing. It's just for fun and I really enjoy it. It keeps me fit and I have made

some really good friends through street dance. I'm also interested in staying in touch with people via the Internet, including staying in touch with Pierre, who was my French exchange partner.'

ACTION

Think of any ways that your hobbies and interests would help you in the job you are applying for.

You've already read about Natalie in previous chapters. She wants to work as a customer service assistant. Natalie's hobbies are jewellery making, shopping and spending times with her friends or watching *Charmed* on DVD. So let's see how we can weave her hobbies into an answer to this question.

'As a customer service assistant you need to be sociable, good with people and provide a good level of service to customers. Because I like shopping I go into a lot of shops and see how some sales staff are much friendlier than others. I'm also good with detail; you need to be for using tweezers to put together jewellery. So what interests me in this job is that I can use some of the skills I already have – an interest in people and attention to detail.'

Working with others

Questions about you will include questions about how you work with others. In particular questions will focus on the kinds of people you work best with and those that are more difficult.

What kind of people do you work best with?

They are probably asking this question to see how well you will fit in with your colleagues and customers. If it's true, you could tell them that you work well with all sorts of people but you work best with people who want to get on and do a good job. You could also remind them of different people that you have worked with and how you have got on with all of them. This anticipates the next question.

ACTION

What will you say to the question 'What kinds of people do you work best with?'

What sort of people do you find it difficult to work with?

It's easy to be honest and to talk about the sort of people you find difficult, but it's unlikely to do you any favours if you are too honest. What the interviewer wants to know is that you get on with all sorts of people and don't find anyone difficult, so make sure to say something like:

> 'I've not had a real problem getting on with anyone. I know some people can be a bit miserable or very sharp in the way they talk but I just do my best to accept them for what they are.'

> 'At college we were given a project and put into groups of four. Three of us worked well together and all got involved but the fourth person just wanted to leave us to do all the work and just mucked about when we were working together and didn't do their tasks for the second meeting. We all found it very frustrating and ended up doing their share of the work as nothing we could say would make them do anything.'

This second answer is interesting, it was unresolved, the group let the person get away with not working, so this might well result in a follow-up question, asking you what you learnt from this.

TIP Be ready for a follow-up question. It's always useful to think of what you have learnt from a particular situation.

A danger question!

What was the biggest weakness of your boss?
What irritates you about your colleagues?

These questions are designed to trap you, to see if you will 'bad mouth' people you know. Don't say anything negative. Instead let the interviewer know that your boss treated you well, was good at his job and you didn't notice any weaknesses. Also, nothing irritated you about your colleagues. You all got on really well together.

Questions about your personal qualities

People have some or many personal qualities that are relevant to work and these may be useful for you to discuss. Below is a list of important qualities that the employer will be looking for in the winning candidate.

I'm not expecting you to be able to give examples against all of these areas; you will develop these over time to come. So look at the list below.

- Commitment to the task
- Dependable
- Time management
- Self motivated
- Drive and energy
- Initiative
- Flexibility
- Adaptable
- Problem solving
- Logical thinker

- Willingness to learn
- Self confident
- Communication skills
- Team worker
- Numerical skills

It can be useful to write your examples down so you can refer to them as part of your preparation or interview. For example:

- when you write down 'dependable', you may have been thinking of the two years you worked at a newsagent starting at 5a.m. to mark up the papers for delivery, never missing a day due to illness or even being late.
- you could confirm your numerical skills because of your excellent skills demonstrated through getting A* at GCSE Maths.

ACTION

Try to think of situations where you have demonstrated each of these skills in a professional or social capacity. Write it down so you can refer to it later.

Strengths and weaknesses

Interviewers will always ask you about your strengths and weaknesses, sometimes this will be done as a straightforward question – 'What are your strengths and weaknesses?' – so you need to prepare and you can be 95% certain that the question will come up.

At other times they might ask you the question in a different way by asking you what other people would say about you. For example:

- What would a previous supervisor say are your strongest points?
- How would your teacher describe you?
- What would your friends say about you?

If you can remember what they have said you could say 'I did ask my friends this question and they said ...'

Strengths are the things you are good at and can include abilities, skills and personal qualities.

Answering the question about your strengths should be easy as you already know what you are good at. You may have quite a few different strengths and skills, and some of them could be a bit unusual – 'I am very good at baton twirling.' This is unlikely to be relevant to the job but using it as an example would be fine and would certainly make you stand out. You are more likely, however, to refer to more work-related strengths such as creativity or attention to detail.

Wherever possible talk about strengths that relate to the job you are applying for.

Many jobs involve working with people so it will help to have a strength relating to your interpersonal skills. If you are looking for an administration job, talk about your attention to detail.

ACTION

Make a note of your top strengths.

So why not think about your strengths, and not just one but three or four. Interviewers will often ask for three examples. If you are able you could include examples from different parts of your life — so one from a hobby, another from any work experience you may have and another related to your studies.

TALK TO FRIENDS, FAMILY AND PEOPLE YOU WORK WITH FOR EXAMPLES

Sometimes it can be hard to think of your strengths so you might like to ask people that know you. Definitely ask people that know you well including friends, family and people you work with (if you are working).

Make a note of what they say below

Friends say

Family members say

People I work with say

Prepare your answers

There are some areas that are likely to come up at interview so see if you can put any of the strengths you have already noted under these next areas.

We looked at these in Chapter 6 where we looked at competency based questions. You might like to read that chapter and your answers again and then fill in some examples of strengths in the boxes below.

MAKE A NOTE OF EXAMPLES OF WHEN YOU HAVE DISPLAYED THE FOLLOWING STRENGTHS

Ability to prioritise

Problem solving

Working under pressure

Getting on with a range of people

Positive attitude

Being organised

It will really help you if you have thought about what you can say before you read through what other people have said. Once you have done this read what others have said below.

Ability to prioritise

'When I was at college I had a number of pieces of work to complete alongside practise for the football team. I made sure I put all the dates in my diary and then estimated how long each task would take so I could get everything done. I never used to be so organised but after having too much to do with revision I learnt a way to make sure I would never miss a deadline again.'

Problem solving

'A problem I solved was helping out at our village fête. Some people didn't turn up and we had a spare stand. The organiser was getting very stressed as there would be this space. I had a think and then suggested that I turn it into an information stand on climate change and went home, printed out some details and put them on the table. I also got some school friends to come along and talk to people about this.'

Working under pressure

'The most pressurised period of my life was studying for my A levels alongside working after school on a couple of days, and Saturday at a café. I had to really manage my time well and cut out on doing anything that was non essential.'

Getting on with a range of people

You can't just say 'I'm good with people', the interviewer will want to know what sort of people and what specifically are you good at. One way to answer is to say:

'I like people and whether it is students I study with, customers at the charity shop I help out at or the customers when I used to work at the Nail Bar, every one has said that I am friendly and easy to get on with.'

Positive attitude

'I've been brought up to have a positive attitude. That means that when things go wrong I look for ways to put things right rather than to concentrate on the problems. I think that being creative helps me to identify different options.'

Being organised

'I'm very well organised and manage my time between studies and a part-time job at (a fast food restaurant). We have many targets around the work we do and my organising skills help me to do exactly what is required to meet these targets such as ....'

What are your best achievements?

This question is asking you about what you are good at but in a slightly different way than asking you about you strengths. The interviewer wants to know what you have achieved. In the early stages of your career you are not expected to have achieved major achievements at work, and so you can certainly use an example from school or your hobbies.

'I am most proud of winning an award for not having a single day off sick while I was at school.'

'One of my best achievements is to have produced some flyers for use by a local charity – I made them very eye catching and they were really pleased with them. Would you like to see one?'

The achievement question could also be asked in a slightly different way, but you could use any of the above examples here as well.

Tell me about a time when you were best at something

'At college we had a project to create a web site. It could have been on anything but I decided to create an e-commerce site. This involved me creating products to sell, T-shirts, badges and posters. Nobody else had thought about creating a site to sell something and my tutor said that mine definitely had the potential to make money!'

What are your weaknesses?

Having spoken about your strengths, the interviewer will also ask you about your weaknesses. This can be a direct question, 'What are your weaknesses?' Or it might be less direct such as, 'What would your friends say if I asked them about your faults?'

This question is being asked to see if you are arrogant, 'I really don't think I have any weaknesses', whether you know yourself, 'I've never thought about that before' and also how you are working to overcome a weakness.

You can talk about a weakness that you have worked to overcome with an answer such as

'I can get impatient with people who don't make it clear what they want, so I've learned to listen more deliberately.'

TIP You could choose one example that is also seen as strength, but don't only choose these sorts of examples.

'I am sometimes impatient which means I get on and do something myself rather than to wait for someone else to do it.'

'I sometimes get so engrossed in a task I forget about other things and end up working late.'

'I do get frustrated with people who are late.'

'I could be seen as too much of a perfectionist as I want to get everything right.'

'I'm finding it hard to learn how to drive and I have to take more lessons than my friends, but I'm getting there.'

The third approach is to either say that you don't know of any weakness that could affect your ability to do the job, or that you talk about a previous weakness and how you have overcome it, in which case you would say something like:

'I was very shy and tongue tied whenever I had to answer the phone, but then I talked about this with my supervisor who set up some practise sessions and one-to-one coaching and I'm now much more confident and have got some good feedback from customers.'

'When I was younger I would say that I knew what I needed to do and then later realise that I didn't and would find myself struggling. I found it hard to ask for help, but I've realised that people don't mind helping out and it does mean that I'm learning and improving. I'm still not 100% on this, but I'm getting there and most of the time I do ask.'

Finally you could refer to a weakness you are trying to overcome such as:

'I'm not as good with Dreamweaver as other software but I am trying to use it more.'

Questions about your education

When you haven't had much work experience, you will be asked more questions about your education and your time at school, college or university. Let's look at three questions you could be asked.

Why did you choose your A levels or college course?

When we don't have many examples from work to draw on an interviewer will ask questions about choices we have made through our studies. So for example if you chose a subject, such as music, this could be because you have always been interested in both playing and composing music. If you chose to study Spanish it could be because you went on holiday to Spain with your family and since then have travelled in other Spanish speaking countries.

> 'I studied maths because it is my best subject and I enjoy the problem solving element.'

> 'I chose to study for a BTEC in Business Studies as I though this would give me a good basis of business skills that would be directly transferable to a job like this one.'

Which part of your education do you see as relevant to this position?

We have been reading about Tom who studied multimedia and wanted to work in graphic design. It's quite easy for him to see a direct link between his course and the job he is applying for so he is able to say something like:

> 'I chose the course as I was interested in both computers and design. What I've enjoyed is learning to use different software and it has helped me to realise that it is the graphic design/ illustrating element that really interests me. This is going to help me right away as I'm familiar with some of the software you use such as Illustrator and Photoshop.'

> 'We had to do quite a lot of group work at college and from this I've learnt a lot about working as part of a team and getting on with people who differ in their approach to work from mine'.

Flexibility and ability to get to work on time

Many jobs now involve unsociable hours and also a need for flexibility to meet the needs of the customer. Gone are the days when people worked 8 hour days when there was little work to be done in the first and last hour. Now companies want to make sure that people are only employed when needed.

So think about how you would respond to these questions

- Are you willing to work overtime?
- Are you willing to work nights? Weekends?

It makes it so much easier for a manager to have a flexible workforce; the company saves money as they don't need to have more people than neces-sary working at the quiet times. They also don't want to have people who will only work set hours and are not able to come in at short notice etc. However, you don't want to say you are fully flexible if you are not, and if a company really wants you they can be understanding and meet your require-ments, as long as you are something special.

ARE YOU FLEXIBLE?

You might not want to but would you be willing to work early mornings or late evenings? For example if you are applying for a job at McDonald's you might find that it's open between 5a.m. and 2a.m. – are you able to do the very early starts and the very late finishes? Are there some times you definitely don't want to work?

Tied in with this is checking out about your access to transport. If like Tom you wanted to work in a bar, how will you get home when your shift finishes at 1a.m. if you don't have your own car? Other jobs may start at 8a.m. and again an interviewer would want to know you can get there on time for your shift. Be ready to confirm to your interviewer that getting to work early or getting home very late is not a problem.

Future plans and goals

When we are applying for our first job most of us haven't given much thought at all to where we want to be in a few years time, we just want to get a job and start earning some money. So when you are asked a question such as 'Where do you see yourself in 2–5 years time?' you might be unsure of what to say.

What the interviewer wants to know is that you plan to stay for a while. They don't want to have to replace you in a few months time because you have found something better. Stress your strengths and say how you can use them in this job. You could also say that as long as you can develop and grow you see yourself staying for quite some time. Do not talk about how this is something you will do until you find something better!

Goal setting and achieving goals is something many interviewers want to hear about at interview, so think about what you can say. This could be either about a goal you set your self and achieved or a goal you have planned for the future.

ACTION

What will you say? Write down your future plans and goals.

What are your short and long term goals?

This should link with the job you are applying for. If you want to be a retail manager, a job as a sales assistant is a first step; but if you want to be a legal executive why are you applying for a job in a nursery? You could respond with something like:

> 'My short term goal is to join a company where I will be challenged and be able to learn new things. One of my longer term goals in to grow with the company and move into management.'

'In the short term it's to get a job where I can
apply my skills and experience to help a company
provide an excellent service to customers.
In the longer term I'm looking to gain more
responsibility.'

Think about some of the goals you have and how you could achieve them.
They could be something like the example below.

'I could barely swim, so when I was on a family
holiday in Tenerife, I decided to set about learning.
I spent several hours a day swimming in the pool
– I began on the first day swimming half a width
and after a week I was up to 2 lengths. By the
time we came home I could swim 10 lengths and
I'm really proud of myself, I just kept on doing a
little bit more each time. I think that this approach
would be useful for any goal I set myself in the
future.'

Now make a note of your own goals.

8

Questions you can ask

Over to you … Questions to ask at the end of the interview.

At the end of the interview, you will be asked if you have any questions. By the end of this chapter you will

- understand why you need to ask questions
- understand what not to ask
- have a plan for how to develop questions
- know how to use questions to emphasise your strengths
- have a great finale to the interview.

Why you need to ask questions

When you apply for a job you don't just send a CV but also a covering letter, it enhances your application. In the same way when you go for an interview you don't just answer the questions asked but also ask questions yourself. It enhances the impression you give.

The main part of the interview is lead by the interviewer. They know what they want to find out and ask questions to hear what you have to say.

It is then the 'Over to you' stage of the interview where you get a chance to ask questions. This gives you a chance to again stand out from the other applicants. You want to have some questions prepared to reinforce that you have done your research and that you are interested in the company. **You must have questions available.** If you pass on this option and say that everything has been covered it makes for a weak ending.

Don't be a candidate who says that 'everything has been covered'. Demonstrate you have thought about this job and ask some relevant questions.

What not to ask

There is a difference between what you want to know and the questions you want to ask. Of course you want to know how much you will get paid, what your holiday entitlements are and if there are any perks to working for the company (discounts off goods etc.) but if you ask questions that relate to these areas the focus is on what you want to gain rather than telling them even more good things about how you are perfect for the job.

Once you get the job offer you can then find out the answers to basic details about the terms and conditions of the job.

A plan for how to develop questions

Questions can **relate to the company,** things you have found out about them from their web site, company literature and an Internet search. You may have already been asked a question by the interviewer about the company but you could also ask a question to demonstrate the research you have done on the company. Rather than a general question, link it to something you have read. For example:

> 'I read on your web site that you have recently launched a new range of beauty products in addition to your medical equipment. I'm interested in why the company did this.'

Questions about **the actual job** – what you would be doing and how the vacancy has come up, who would be your manager, who you would be working with. Asking why the vacancy arose means you will know if this is a new position, or if you are replacing someone. You might like to find out whether they were promoted or left.

'Can you tell me a bit more about the job role?'

You may not have found out enough about the actual job, so if the interviewer hasn't given enough detail, do ask. You can't be expected to say yes to a job you don't know about.

'Who would be my manager?'

It's good to find out if your manager will be the person who has interviewed you or if it will be somebody else. If someone else you might like to ask if you could meet them.

Questions to **show your enthusiasm** – what you really love about their products/company and could include asking to be shown around. You might also like to ask if there is any opportunity to study for relevant qualifications.

'Could I have a look around before I left?'

This shows enthusiasm and even if they say no, nothing has been lost.

'If I am successful, can you tell me what happens in the first week?'

This will help you find out if there is a structured induction plan or if you are going to be left to get on with it.

'If I was to be offered the job, what preparation could I do?'

This demonstrates your enthusiasm, interest and helps them to visualise you in the role.

How to use questions to emphasise your strengths

Some of these questions could be about your background. You may have some really great personal qualities, abilities and the questions asked haven't given you a chance to discuss these.

So have ready questions to bring out something in your background that you haven't been able to get across.

ACTION

Prepare a relevant question for each of your strengths. Go back and look at your strengths in the last chapter and think of a question you could ask which relates to each.

For example, if you are strong in problem solving you could ask a question like:

'Is there a need to solve problems in the job, I'm asking because this is one of my strengths and I've ...'

Where you give a specific example or

'Do you encourage staff to come up with new ideas? The reason I'm asking is because ...'

Don't think you have to remember all of these questions; it's absolutely fine to have them written on a pad which you can refer to when the interviewer moves into this phase.

Even in the worst case scenario when all your questions have already been covered, as you pull out your pad to check the interviewer will see that you had them listed down and you can say that everything has been covered.

A great finale to the interview

Once you have asked about four questions you can thank the interviewer for answering your questions, tell them how much you are interested in the company and its products/services and that you are very interested in the job. You can then ask:

'What are the next steps?'

You ideally want to find out when you will hear back from them. This means that you can contact them again if you don't hear from them.

The interviewer will then probably thank you for coming. It is now a case of saying goodbye, not just to the interviewer or interviewers but also to say goodbye to the receptionist and anyone else you met as you arrived.

9

Dealing with weak spots in your application

The focus of this book is on how to answer interview questions and we have looked at these in depth. However, as a first-time job seeker you may be concerned about your application, so let's see how to address them. By the end of this chapter you will be clear on what to do:

- when you don't really know what the job involves
- when you lack relevant experience
- when you don't know much about the industry/company
- when it's a few months since you left school/college and you haven't had a job

So read on to find out how to address these areas.

You don't really know what the job involves

The job advert will include details on the job requirements, but you can also find out more. There are some really useful web sites that can help such as

http://careersadvice.direct.gov.uk/helpwithyourcareer/jobprofiles/

If you look up details on the job that interests you, you can use this to ensure that your application covers the relevant skills and knowledge needed, from all areas of your life and also you can read about what you would be doing in the job, so you can think about relevant examples and be ready to discuss these at interview.

For example if you are interested in applying for work as a museum assistant, the web site above will describe the skills and knowledge you will need:

- good communication and 'people' skills
- customer service skills
- a responsible attitude and awareness of security issues
- the ability to remain alert over long periods of time
- the ability to react quickly in an emergency.

You can then use this to look for relevant examples against these areas.

You lack relevant experience

Many of us haven't already done the job we are applying for but we have what is known as 'transferable skills'. This means that we can look at what is required and use examples from what we have already done.

TIP   Transferable skills are not only from a job, they can be from hobbies and school as well.

Using the example above, as a museum assistant the job requires people who have a number of different skills and personal qualities. Let's look at other places you could have gained these.

Good communication and 'people' skills – you could choose examples from presenting to the class, voluntary work, or talking to the public on a campaigning stand for an issue you believe in.

Customer service skills – think about any time you have been helpful for others and also think about examples you have noticed of good customer service. Your teacher could be seen as a customer.

> 'I think I would be successful in customer service as I get on really well with people, and I'm very interested in helping people by finding out more about their problems and getting them sorted. I'm warm and friendly and enjoy working as part of a team. I'm also very interested in learning and

developing and willing to undertake study if it makes me more effective in my work and helps me for the future.'

A responsible attitude and awareness of security issues – many people may find this hard to answer and you may not have specific examples to demonstrate this. It is asking for an 'awareness of security issues' and so you can refer to what you know about not leaving bags unattended, the need to look out for suspicious packages and the importance of checking people before they enter buildings. Responsible can be covered by, for example, you dealing with the subs for members of the cricket team or collecting money for charity fund raising.

The ability to remain alert over long periods of time – this is being asked as working in a museum can involve a lot of watching and there is a need to pay close attention to people. Previous experience as a life guard would be ideal, as you would have needed to be observant but you may also have done playground duty as part of your prefect duties and that would be a relevant example.

The ability to react quickly in an emergency – an example could include: if you had been involved in a fire drill that would be relevant, especially if you had helped others to leave the building promptly.

TIP Take the time to think about relevant examples from your life. Talk with other people that know you to see if they can help you to think beyond the day to day things you do.

When you don't have previous experience in the sort of work you are applying for

You have read about Tom earlier who was looking for a first job in graphic design. He had got short-listed and so his lack of work experience was not a problem. He could respond to this question with something like:

'I know I'm not an expert in all the different software programs, so if it's essential for me to become more experienced in any particular area I'd be keen to undertake any training courses, learn on the job and also practise at home to get more familiar. I've shown through my time at college how I am quick at picking up new software.'

And if you are Chris, who had a Saturday job for 6 months and now wants a job as an accounts clerk you could say:

'I may not have worked in an accounts department, but I got a grade B at Maths GCSE and am confident with figures. In the shop I would balance daily returns so am used to working with numerical data. I'd also check stock in so that's shown how I can pay attention to detail. Plus I'm a quick learner and am really interested in engineering, so working for an engineering company means I am interested in the products you make.'

TIP   You can also gain relevant experience by asking if you can undertake unpaid work experience or to shadow somebody who is doing the job.

You don't know much about the industry/company

There are many companies out there and most of us don't really know what they do, but if you are applying for a job you need to find out and you can do this by looking on the company web site and also doing an Internet search to see what else you can find out.

When it's a few months since you left school/college and you haven't had a job

An interviewer wants to know what you been doing since you left school/college. Interviewers don't want to think that you have been doing nothing.

While you search for your first job look for ways you can get to do some voluntary work.

- If you are interested in retail or customer service roles, voluntary work at a charity shop would be useful.
- If you want to use your computer skills in a job you could also do this for a charity. For example, Oxfam has some charity shops which just sell books and they want people to keep their database up to date and upload books for sale on Amazon and eBay.
- If you are after a more physical job, then helping out your elderly neighbours could be seen as relevant work experience, if you do things like mowing lawns, gardening and simple repairs.
- If you want to work in child care you could help out with a family, supporting a mum to look after her younger children or you could volunteer at a primary school and listen to younger children reading.
- If it is social care work you could arrange to go to an old people's home and listen to their stories.
- If you may need to be familiar with a particular type of software, or knowledge of a foreign language would be helpful then you could study from home or do a part-time course at college.

ACTION

If you are searching/looking for your first job, what could you do that will enhance your CV? Use the list above to develop a plan for what you can do.

10
After the interview

There's a phrase 'it ain't over till the fat lady sings' which means that we shouldn't assume the outcome of some activity until it has actually finished. There are things you can do after the interview to increase your chance of success and this is what will be covered in this final chapter:

- the post interview review
- the follow up (thank-you) letter
- what to do if you get the 'regret' letter.

Post interview review

After the interview it is good to take some time to review how it went and to make a few notes about what was discussed.

Most people feel such a sense of relief that an interview is over that they just want to clear their head, relax and unwind and try to forget about it. One way to stand out from the majority is to wait 5 or 10 minutes before you go into unwind mode and instead to do a review of how the interview went. This means that you will have learnt from this and if you don't get the job offer you will have some good suggestions for what to do differently next time.

TIP While you can wait and review the interview when you get home, you might have forgotten some of the information. So try and make a note as soon as you can.

First, think about as much detail as you can about the person or people you met and what you found out. Can you remember and make a note of:

- the interviewer's full name and title?
- who else from the company you meet? What were their names?
- exactly what does the job entail?
- any mention of salary? What was said?

The next thing to do is to review how you think you came across. Sometimes, especially if we think we haven't done well, we just want to forget about it but that means we miss out on thinking about what we did well and also what could have gone a little better. We often have to go through several interviews before we get a job offer, and we do improve! So make a note of what went well and also any areas where you could do better.

Quiz

Use the questions below to help you review how you did at interview

Was I in the right frame of mind?

Definitely   Ok   Not really

Perhaps you had received some bad news that day, or you were worrying about something. If we are distracted by something it means it is hard concentrating so don't beat yourself up if this was something outside of your control.

Was my eye contact right, did I smile?

Definitely   Ok   Not really

Making warm and friendly eye contact helps to build rapport but sometimes we are shy and find it difficult. If you struggled to do this, remember to look at the space just above their nose and practise smiling. It doesn't have to be a huge grin!

Did I prepare myself for the interview?

Definitely   Ok   Not really

This book has talked about the importance of preparation; sometimes people think they can 'wing it' but this is a dangerous approach to take. It's much better to do your research on the company and to have some clear examples about yourself.

Did I demonstrate I knew enough about the company?

Definitely   Ok   Not really

Were you able to demonstrate what you knew or were you kicking yourself when they asked you what you knew about the company? It's really important to do some research, as it shows your interest in the company.

Was I a good candidate?

Definitely   Ok   Not really

Did I answer questions in enough detail? Did I have questions ready to ask? There is a bit of a game to the interview and you need to have performed your role well.

Having seen the people in the company, was I appropriately dressed?

Definitely   Ok   Not really

It's always a good idea to dress smartly at interview so were you looking smart enough? It doesn't have to be a suit; an open neck shirt with chinos, or skirt and jumper for a woman, should look good for many jobs. Do make sure your clothes are clean and pressed with clean polished shoes.

Did I answer the questions thoroughly?

Definitely   Ok   Not really

It can be tempting to answer just yes or no to certain questions but you do need to give more detail. Did you give enough?

Did I emphasise how I can use my skills in this job?

Definitely   Ok   Not really

We're back to research again and knowing how you can relate your skills and education to the job. There have been plenty of suggestions for how to know your skills and answer relevant questions were you able to do so.

Was the interviewer interested and involved in what I was saying?

Definitely   Ok   Not really

It's the tone and pace of our voice along with what we actually say that makes people interested in listening to us. If you aren't sure how you sound, record yourself and listen critically.

Did I answer the questions in a way that stressed my most important characteristics? Was the interviewer clear on my strengths, ability and suitability for the job?

Definitely   Ok   Not really

Being clear on your strengths helps you to answer questions in a way that lets the interviewer know how great you are.

Did I present an accurate and favourable picture of myself?

Definitely   Ok   Not really

Did I avoid putting my foot in it and giving examples of where I wasn't so good? Remember you mustn't tell people more than they need to know and don't be too truthful about your weaknesses.

Did I look my best?

Definitely   Ok   Not really

It's not just about the clothes you wear but also if your hair is clean and styled and any makeup is discreet If you have piercings did you reduce them to a minimum unless you were sure it would be acceptable?

Was I relaxed and in control of myself?

Definitely   Ok   Not really

Or was I nervous and unsure? If so read this book again carefully and do the exercises to help you prepare for next time.

Did I appear confident and show genuine enthusiasm?

Definitely   Ok   Not really

Interviewers want candidates who are confident and enthusiastic for the job. If you are only applying for the job because you think you have to and are not very interested in it then you are unlikely to show enthusiasm. You don't demonstrate interest and enthusiasm solely by what you say but also by how you say it.

Did I talk just the right amount, neither too much nor too little?

Definitely   Ok   Not really

There's a need for balance – you must answer the questions in sufficient details but also allow some space so the interviewer can ask further questions. If you just answer the absolute minimum you have not really demonstrated much aptitude for the job.

Did my answers satisfy the interviewer?

Definitely   Ok   Not really

If your answers to questions were a bit vague, the interviewer may have asked a follow-up question but they may also only give you one chance to answer. You must listen to the question and answer it as best you can.

Was I able to discuss my strengths and weaknesses?

Definitely   Ok   Not really

You should have these prepared in advance, these are the easy questions! Were you ok with them? If not do a practise session with a friend.

Did I show that I was listening to the interviewer?

Definitely   Ok   Not really

Active listening means looking attentively, with some nods as the interviewer asks questions. It's not avoiding eye contact and looking a little shifty! Remember, if you struggle with this, to look at the space between their eyes, you shouldn't feel as self conscious about it.

Did I say why I wanted to work for the organisation?

Definitely   Ok   Not really

If they didn't ask you the question, you needed to make sure you covered this at the end when it was your time to ask questions.

Does it still sound fresh, despite having to regularly repeat it?

Definitely   Ok   Not really

If you have had quite a few interviews you many find that you have answered the same question over and over again. You have to sound enthusiastic and make your answer sound like it is the first time you have said it.

Did I ask some good questions at the end?

Definitely   Ok   Not really

The previous chapter gives details on a number of questions you could ask, plus how to ask questions which can demonstrate your strengths, so you should have done well. If not, what happened?

Scoring

Let's see how you have done. Give yourself 2 points for each time you chose Definitely, 1 point for each time you chose OK and 0 for any time you chose Not Really.

Total up your scores.

40–44

If you have rated yourself accurately you have done all you can possibly do to be a great interviewee.

30–39

You should do well, but there are some areas where you feel less confident. What do you need to do to help you to improve?

20–29

It looks like you need to do quite a bit of work to help you to come across well. I suggest you re-read this book and make sure that you do all the exercises to help you to prepare.

19 or fewer

If you have significant improvements to make you need to re-read this book carefully, but it might also be nerves that have affected your performance. You might find it valuable to do a mock interview to overcome your nerves and may benefit from some career coaching.

Other questions to ask yourself

Which questions did I handle well?

Make a note of the questions you handled well and do congratulate yourself.

Which questions did I handle poorly?

The questions in this book will have been great preparation. Did they help and did you think before you answered or was there a bit of panic and you maybe gave a vague and woolly answer? If you can remember, make a note of the difficult questions and think about how you would answer better next time

Did I find out all I needed to?

Were there questions you forgot to ask? Make sure to write them down next time.

Would I like to work for that organisation?

You might be very keen to get just any job, but what do you think of it now you have been there? Sometimes we get a bad feeling about a place or the people, so think carefully if you would want the job if it was offered to you.

What additional research do I need to do before a subsequent interview?

Sometimes you will have more than one interview so if you are likely to get a second interview, think about some of the questions you may be asked next time.

Follow up with a thank-you letter

One way to leave a memorable impression is to send a follow up letter to say thank-you.

TIP

> Very few candidates send a thank-you letter and it can give you the edge that makes you stand out from the rest.

The choice of who gets the job may be between you and one other person and so a letter might make the difference. When I suggest this to clients they often hesitate, and think that an employer will think they are 'sucking up' but most employers are very pleased to get a thank-you letter as it reinforces your interest in the job.

Sometimes you may be interviewed by more than one person in which case send letters to each person making small changes so the letters are not identical, should they all compare letters.

Sending a thank-you letter gives you a chance to remind the interviewer of your strengths and also provides an example of your written communication skills. If you hand write a letter it is obviously personalised but if your hand writing isn't very clear it's better to type it but do include a personal signature.

> You could email, but a posted letter stands out, people get so many emails that yours could just get lost, and a posted letter is quite unusual nowadays. However if you can't get it there for the next day it is better to email, but you can still follow up with a posted letter.

Your thank you letter can also cover any areas of weakness, reservations or concerns that you think might stop you getting a job. So in the letter you can refer to your strengths and personal characteristics and how these can over compensate for any areas of weakness.

> If you live locally, why not hand deliver a thank-you letter later that day?

Here is a structure for a thank-you letter, followed by a typical letter. Use this as a guide, but make it personal to you, you don't want an employer to receive identical letters from you and someone else.

Structure of a thank-you letter

Paragraph 1
Thank-you for interviewing me for the position of xxx on (date).

Paragraph 2
Remind them why you want the job and what you have to offer the company. If you think the interview didn't go as well as it could you could provide some relevant information.

Paragraph 3
Thank the interviewer. Say how you may be contacted if they need additional information.

Let's have a look at a typical letter:

> Thank-you for the opportunity to attend for interview last Tuesday for the role of customer service assistant. During the interview you asked why I would be a good candidate for this job and I think I could have given clearer reasons. I've thought about how my strengths are well suited to this job and these are _____.
>
> I enjoyed meeting you and can confirm that I am very interested in working with THE COMPANY. I hope to hear from you very soon.

Before you print and post or email your letter, read it through carefully and check that there are no typos and it reads grammatically correct.

> Julie told me that after she had started a new job, her boss told her that he had been undecided between Julie and another candidate, and it was receiving the thank-you letter which made the difference.

Waiting

For some jobs you will hear how you got on very quickly, sometimes by phone call the next day, but for other jobs it can take time before you hear something. This is usually for companies that are recruiting for a number of jobs at once as they want to make all the decisions together. This is why it's good to find out at the interview when you are likely to hear something as if you haven't heard by then you can certainly phone up to find out what is happening.

Decision making

If you have been interviewed you will get told if you have or haven't got the job. You will either get a letter telling you that you were successful (sometimes it could be a phone call with confirmation in writing) or you may get the letter telling you that you were not successful – the regret letter.

What to do if you get a regret letter

If you get a regret letter; 'We regret to inform you . . .,' it could be for one of five reasons:

1 **There was not a good match between you and the job.** In this case, the regret letter is a positive outcome. You would not have liked that job anyway.
2 **You do not have the right background for this job.** You may not yet be ready for this job. You perhaps applied for a job as executive officer when you should have applied for an admin level job.
3 **There was a good match but you simply did not interview well.** You need to spend time on interview practise.
4 **There were a lot of very good candidates.** There may have been more than one person who was capable of doing the job. The final decision may have been based on factors outside your control. The person who got the job may have been an internal candidate or had something extra to offer.

5 This could also be because the **head office wants to fill the vacancy but the local branch has no intention of filling it,** or the job has already been offered to someone and the ad was to 'go through the motions'. Another possibility is the job is being downsized and will go to someone the company wants to make redundant.

Whatever you think is the reason you didn't get the job, contact the company and seek feedback from them.

Finally, even if you do not get an offer, you can still write one last letter. The person who has been offered the job may turn it down and this could lead to an offer for you. Plus, it will definitely leave a favourable impression.

A reply to the regret letter

You could send a letter thanking the interviewer for taking the time to consider you for the position and to wish the new employee every success. Say that you would be happy to be considered for the position should it become vacant in the future. Quite regularly, a new employee leaves quite quickly as it hasn't worked out for them and this would bring you to the top of the list when a new person is being considered.

> Thank-you for your kind call to tell me that the job has been filled. Of course I'm disappointed not to be selected for the position; but I want to wish you and your new employee well.
>
> Once again, thank-you for the consideration you have given my application for this position. Should there be a vacancy in the future, I hope you will keep me in mind and contact me.
>
> In the meantime if you are able to give me some feedback on how I could improve my interview performance for next time I would find it very helpful.

You can see that this letter asks for feedback on how they came across at interview as this should be helpful for further interviews. A few companies will provide feedback to all, but that is a small minority of companies. Other companies will refuse to give feedback to anyone. It is well worth asking so do make contact and don't be afraid to follow up if you don't hear anything.

You've got the job!

If you have got the job, well done! It's wonderful news to hear that you have been offered a job. You may be told there and then, right after your interview. You might get a phone call a day or so later or the result may come by letter. Often the bigger the company, the longer they take to get back to you. **If you are told face to face, or by phone make sure that you sound enthusiastic, to reinforce that they made the right choice.** You may well have some questions to ask, so make sure to ask, they expect people to have specific questions now. So you could say something like:

They will probably tell you that you will get confirmation in writing including details on pay, holidays etc.

> Thank-you so much, I'm really thrilled. Can you let me know what happens next?
>
> Thank-you so much, can you give me more details on the job offer or will I receive something in writing in the next day or so?

You don't have to accept the job right away, especially if you think another company may make you an offer or if you aren't 100% certain that you want the job. So it is fine to ask for a day or so to review the offer, waiting to get the results in writing will give you some extra time.

When you have made your decision, phone to accept and make sure to sound enthusiastic on the phone. Then confirm your acceptance in writing.

Of course, you may decide to turn an offer down. If you do, do so quickly and send a letter which keeps the possibility of you getting in touch again in the future.

Thank-you for offering me a position as a Marketing Assistant with Guardian Consulting. I found our discussions during the interview process helpful to learn more about the details of this position. I appreciated the time you allowed me to consider your offer.

Throughout the interview process, I confirmed my initial impressions of Guardian Consulting as an outstanding organisation. After considerable thought about my career goals, I have chosen to accept the offer from an employer based closer to my family.

I'm sorry to have to decline your job offer. This was a difficult decision for me, although I believe it is the right one for me.

I want to thank you for the time and consideration you have given my application. It was a pleasure meeting you and learning more about Guardian Consulting.

One last thing ...

Now that you have worked your way through this book you should be feeling much more confident about the forthcoming interview.

You will be doing numerous interviews in your life and your ability and confidence will develop over the years.

As you apply for jobs you will face competition. Plenty of other people are likely to be applying for the same job – you need to make sure that everything you do is supporting your application.

- Be clear why you are applying for the job. What is it that interests you?
- Make sure your application is targeted at the job advert.
- Find out as much as you can about the company.
- Know your self and your strengths to help you answer the questions.
- Get someone to do a practise interview with you and also get some feedback to help you improve.
- Always review how you did at the end of each interview.
- Don't beat yourself up if you don't get a job offer. Ask for feedback and look for the next job to apply for.

All the very best for your career success

Denise Taylor
www.amazingpeople.co.uk